Mindful Parenting for ADHD

A Guide to Cultivating Calm, Reducing Stress & Helping Children Thrive

MARK BERTIN, MD

New Harbinger Publications, Inc.

Publisher's Note

Distributed in Canada by Raincoast Books

Copyright © 2015 by Mark Bertin

       New Harbinger Publications, Inc.
       5674 Shattuck Avenue
       Oakland, CA 94609
       www.newharbinger.com

Cover design by Amy Shoup
Acquired by Melissa Kirk
Edited by Jasmine Star

Library of Congress Cataloging-in-Publication Data

Bertin, Mark.
  Mindful parenting for ADHD : a guide to cultivating calm, reducing stress, and helping children thrive / Mark Bertin, MD
Foreword by Ari Tuckman, PsyD, MBA.
    pages cm
  Includes bibliographical references.
  ISBN 978-1-62625-179-3 (paperback) -- ISBN 978-1-62625-180-9 (pdf e-book) -- ISBN 978-1-62625-181-6 (epub) 1. Attention-deficit hyperactivity disorder. 2. Child rearing. I. Title.
  RJ506.H9B473 2015
  618.92'8589--dc23

               2015014897

Printed in the United States of America

17   16   15

10 9 8 7 6 5 4 3 2 1   First printing

"In *Mindful Parenting for ADHD*, Mark Bertin provides an essential guide for parents and clinicians. Parents of children with ADHD and clinicians will benefit from Bertin's relatable writing style, examples, research, and easy-to-accomplish suggestions and recommendations. Most importantly, Bertin gives families and clinicians hope."

—**Stephanie Moulton Sarkis, PhD, NCC, LMHC**, psychotherapist and author of five books on ADHD, including *10 Simple Solutions to Adult ADD* (www.stephaniesarkis.com)

"*Mindful Parenting for ADHD* represents a rare blend: a concise and accurate guide to what ADHD is (and is not), an evidence-based resource for families on behavior management and skill enhancement tools for their children, and an introduction to the kinds of mindful practices (including but not limited to meditation) that both calm and focus parents and model thoughtful strategies for their offspring. Difficult and important issues—the adolescent years, working with schools, and decisions about medication—are addressed head on. Sensitive, easy to read, and profound, this book will resonate with families everywhere who hope for both action and reflection in raising their challenging children."

—**Stephen Hinshaw, PhD**, professor of psychology at University of California, Berkeley, professor of psychiatry at University of California, San Francisco, and author of *The ADHD Explosion: Myths, Medication, Money, and Today's Push for Performance*

"This innovative book combines the best of what is known about ADHD, its deficits in executive functioning, and the types of science-based management strategies they require, as well as possible medications to combine with them, along with the latest practices for incorporating mindfulness into everyday life situations, such as parenting. Parents of children with ADHD struggle not only with managing their children but also with far higher levels of parenting stress, depression, anxiety, and marital strife than do typical parents. This combination of mindfulness practices with more traditional behavioral and medical treatments for ADHD is likely to prove exceptionally useful for parents for both stress reduction and improved parent-child relationships."

—**Russell A. Barkley, PhD**, clinical professor of psychiatry and pediatrics, Medical University of South Carolina

"*Mindful Parenting for ADHD* is a gift to lost and overwhelmed parents. Bertin offers a clear, compassionate, comprehensive, and practical guide to parents struggling to find the calm within the seeming chaos of life with a child with ADHD, along with succinct tools for managing it."

—**Christopher Willard, PsyD**, author of *Child's Mind* and *Growing Up Mindful*, Cambridge Health Alliance/Harvard Medical School

"This book is the ultimate gold mine of understanding your child with ADHD in a new and insightful way. Bertin explains how practicing mindfulness changes the way you as a parent see your child through the lens of truly understanding the ADHD experience. You will learn to act instead of react, understand instead of judge, and stay calm instead of banging your head against the wall. Best of all, Bertin gives you specific, easy-to-follow tools for dealing with challenging behaviors. It all comes down to being mindful, and understanding the ADHD brain and the behaviors that are borne from that. A fabulous book for parents looking for a better way to manage their challenging children, as well as for professionals working with these children. I'll be recommending this one to my clients!"

—**Terry Matlen, ACSW**, director of www.ADDconsults.com, and author of *The Queen of Distraction* and *Survival Tips for Women with AD/HD*

"As the parent of a child with ADHD, and as a holistic physician and mindfulness coach who supports many children and families living with ADHD, I find this book an invaluable resource. Every chapter offers simple, doable, and transformative mindfulness practices; practical, achievable action items; grounded perspective; a long-term view; and most importantly, hope and compassion for children and parents living with ADHD."

—**Amy Saltzman, MD**, director of the Association for Mindfulness in Education and author of *A Still Quiet Place*

"Having ADHD can not only be difficult for the child who suffers the consequences of his or her behaviors, but can also place great stress on the family. Parents don't understand why their child acts the way he does, and because they are unsure, they often react in a way that may not always be helpful. That's where Mark Bertin's new book *Mindful Parenting for ADHD* comes in! Within its pages, parents will grow to better understand ADHD and find the tools necessary to respond to their child's behaviors with compassion, as well as structure, using a focused, mindful approach. *Mindful Parenting for ADHD* underscores the need for parents to take care of themselves in order to meet the challenges of parenting a child with ADHD with calm, kindness, and consistency. Written in a reassuring style and filled with easy-to-use worksheets that cover a myriad of topics from setting limits to improving communication or making the most of homework, I wish all parents of children with ADHD could receive the gifts offered in this wonderful book! They and their children would all be the better for it!"

—**Patricia O. Quinn, MD**, developmental pediatrician, Washington, DC, coauthor of *Putting on the Brakes: Understanding and Taking Control of Your ADD or ADHD* and *Understanding Girls with ADHD*, and author of *Attention, Girls! A Guide to Learn All About Your AD/HD*

"Parenting is a very challenging role, and even more so when children have a diagnosis of ADHD. Mark Bertin has written a truly remarkable book that offers numerous strategies to help children with ADHD to become more successful and resilient. Very importantly, he addresses a key issue; namely, that unless parents learn to deal realistically with their own expectations, pressure, and stress, they will not be as effective when helping their children with ADHD to meet the many developmental demands they will face. In a very empathic, easy-to-read style, Bertin provides practical techniques rooted in mindfulness theory that parents can apply in their own lives. This book is a wonderful resource for parents (and I might add for professionals as well)—a resource that will be read and reread as parents enrich their own lives and the lives of their children."

—**Robert Brooks, PhD**, coauthor of *Raising Resilient Children* and *The Power of Resilience: Achieving Balance, Confidence, and Personal Strength in Your Life*

Contents

Foreword

In contrast to years past, we now know a lot about ADHD. The science is well established. There are well-accepted treatment protocols. Teachers have methods to meet the unique needs of students with ADHD.

But for you, a parent trying to figure out how to rescue your child right here, right now, it can be challenging to know what to do. Some behaviors should be addressed, and others should be ignored. Sometimes your child needs you to intervene, and sometimes she needs to figure it out for herself. Things almost always go better when parents keep their cool, but that's easier said than done.

Russell Barkley, PhD, has famously said that ADHD isn't a disorder of knowing what to do; it's a disorder of doing what you know (2010). This certainly applies to those with ADHD, but it also applies to their family members. For you as a parent, it may be too easy to feel like you haven't responded in the best way, even when you know what an ideal response would be. And, unfortunately, all too often parents feel unsure about how best to respond.

This book will help you on both counts: knowing what to do and then doing it. Dr. Bertin does a great job of explaining the ins and outs of ADHD so you can make better-informed decisions. Then, what unequivocally separates this book from others on this topic is his focus on applying these concepts—not under ideal circumstances, but in the messy flow of real life. To this end, Dr. Bertin guides you through simple but powerful mindfulness techniques that will enable you to be the kind of parent you want to be—not perfect, but more than good enough for your child to thrive.

Parenthood in general is a crash course in having flexible expectations, patience, and a willingness to sometimes change course on the fly. It can be quite a balancing act. Because kids with ADHD are often inconsistent and unpredictable, you'll have to be even more careful to maintain balance between being consistent and predictable, on the one hand, so that your child knows what to expect, and recognizing when plan A isn't working and being willing to switch to plan B, on the other. Amazingly, and as you'll soon see, being more mindful and intentional will help you with both of these aspects: sticking with a plan and knowing when to shift from it.

Parenting easy kids is easy (relatively speaking). It's the more challenging kids who force parents to really bring their best selves to the equation. This book will help you become not only a better parent, but also a better person overall. As you work through it, challenge your assumptions. Allow your more worthy habits to survive and replace those that are less productive with behaviors more in line with who you really want to be. If you can do this in challenging moments with your child, you can do it in the rest of your life too.

—Ari Tuckman, PsyD, MBA

Acknowledgments

I'd like to thank Melissa Kirk, Jess Beebe, and everyone at New Harbinger Publications for their support, time, and insightful feedback. I'm also grateful to countless friends and colleagues who both contributed and helped keep me sane, including Cynthia Braun, Candida Fink, Elio Gizzi, Jill Green, Janice Kaplan, Carol Mann, Oren Mason, Amy Saltzman, Steve Salzinger, Jennifer Swanson, Ari Tuckman, Chris Willard, Debora Yost, and Lidia Zylowska. I extend special gratitude to the many mindfulness teachers I've read and encountered in my life. And lastly, thank you to my family and parents for their never-ending support, humor, and wisdom in guiding me, then to now.

Portions of this book were adapted from my blog posts on the Huffington Post and Psychology Today. Thanks to the staff at both websites, as well as many other groups that have supported my work.

Introduction

Your child has ADHD. He impulsively acts out; he struggles in school; he seemingly won't settle down for even one second after you walk in the door to let you catch your breath. A visceral hook grabs hold, and you do the same old thing you've always done: you yell, you retreat, you set another rule, or you bend one. Then you mentally berate yourself for not staying calm or your child for not doing as he was told.

Challenging as it is, we are all capable of being mindful—for example, staying fully aware of something unpleasant and pausing before responding. Avoiding the reality that you'd like something to be different without being proactive about it won't change anything. But while you sort through the next best action to take (or perhaps decide not to say or do anything for a moment), your child will benefit when you drop the often unconscious assumption that life can be any different that it is right now. Your impulsive child is going to be impulsive *today*, even while you work on a longer-term plan for change.

ADHD is far more than a disorder of attention. It influences social skills, communication, morning routines, bedtime, technology use, eating habits, homework, and anything requiring coordination, planning, or foresight. In addition, your child's ADHD affects others around him, especially family members.

In fact, ADHD often creates unproductive patterns in parents' lives. When parents become overly stressed or overwhelmed, that affects their children. None of us are at our best when tapped out. And because ADHD itself increases family stress, it makes it harder for you to manage your child's ADHD, which then amplifies stress further. Incorporating mindfulness into your life can break this draining cycle.

Mindfulness and Your Family

Integrated throughout this book are mindfulness tools for cultivating focus, resilience, and well-being—both yours and your child's. They take advantage of the brain's innate capacity to rewire itself, an ability we all maintain at any age. In ways that support the rest of ADHD care, you'll build skills such as these for yourself and your children:

- Attention and awareness (vs. distractibility and operating on autopilot)

- Responsiveness (vs. reactivity)

- Intentional, creative problem solving (vs. reliance on entrenched habits)

- Open-minded discernment (vs. reflexive judgment)

- Compassion for yourself and others (vs. criticism and impatience)

A centuries-old practice accessible to anyone, mindfulness aims to build various traits that make the ups and downs of life easier to handle. Clinical research has confirmed its benefits, explaining why it's an exponentially growing part of Western psychology and medicine. With mindfulness, you develop an increased capability to balance seeing things as they are with doing everything possible to change what you can, making everyday living more manageable.

Seeing ADHD as it is and realizing its broad and often insidious effects enhances planning and successful outcomes by any measure. As both a parent and a pediatrician specializing in child development and ADHD, I remain awed by the consistency with which mindfulness supports families. Time after time, no matter the cultural background or family dynamic, parents learning mindfulness report concrete changes that make their child's ADHD far easier to overcome.

Parenting books and psychologists often ask parents to do things like stay calm when angry, or approach old problems from entirely new perspectives. Yet all of us have beliefs and assumptions developed over a lifetime, and these habits die hard. As you'll see, practicing mindfulness makes change of this kind easier.

Here is a large part of why practicing mindfulness profoundly changes your family life: addressing ADHD requires perseverance, flexibility, responsiveness, and an ability to find moments of joy and success during challenging times. All of that is much harder to sustain when you're mentally swamped by anger, fear, or exhaustion. By practicing mindfulness, you'll be promoting your own resilience and well-being not only for your own sake, but because your child will benefit.

Using This Book to Support ADHD Care

You're a parent. You're busy. You're already doing your best; no one actively tries to mismanage anything. More importantly, you can't always get everything exactly "right"; there isn't a clear right or wrong to most parenting decisions.

Any plan you create to manage your child's ADHD will have its ups and downs. Sometimes you may forget to follow through. Something may work for a time and then need to be adjusted. This is to be expected in juggling family life, especially when ADHD is involved.

Read the chapters of this book in order, then revisit specific topics as needed. If you put the book down for a while, come back when it's time. Expect the distractions that take you away from your plans, and each time that happens, notice and start again.

Mindful Parenting for ADHD offers detailed advice for managing ADHD—a complex and frequently misunderstood disorder. Getting a handle on ADHD starts with a broad understanding of what ADHD is and how it affects a child's development. This book will explain what you need to know about seeking a quality evaluation to figure out if your child has ADHD, and then address everything from educational planning, communication, and behavior to ADHD's often hidden impacts on everyday life for both young children and teens.

Various mindfulness practices make managing ADHD simpler. Mindfulness exercises will help you develop new approaches specific to each aspect of ADHD, from improving morning routines to collaborating with educators. In short, and as you'll soon discover, mindfulness augments traditional ADHD care each step of the way.

Each chapter emphasizes concise, practical information. Make copies of the action plans included in each chapter and post them prominently as reminders to yourself. When you lose touch with your intentions, whether related to mindfulness or to helping your child, guide yourself back to your path. Along the way, you'll rediscover the health, happiness, and ease every family deserves.

Downloadable Materials

Guided audio meditations, the action plans presented at the end of each chapter, a bonus handout that busts some common ADHD myths, and some of the worksheets in this book are all available for download at the book's website: http://www.newharbinger .com/31793. Just look for the tag "download available."

Chapter 1

First Steps on a Mindful Path to Managing Your Child's ADHD

Read this chapter to...

- Understand how ADHD, as a medical disorder, affects children and their parents

- Sort out whether your child has ADHD

- Recognize that knowing that your child has (or does not have) ADHD benefits your family, separate from any discussion of treatment

- Support your family with your own mindfulness practice

I f you're reading these words, you or someone you know has raised a question about your child. Maybe he's always running into the street, never seems to listen to you on the first try, alienates other children, overeats, or is struggling in school. Perhaps he's having a hard time focusing on play or on schoolwork. Facing your concerns is likely an overwhelming and stressful experience and probably not at all what you pictured for yourself as a parent.

Sorting through what, if anything, needs to happen next may be equally daunting. Questions lead to more questions, doubts to more doubts:

- *Who should I talk to about my questions?*

- *Do I even need to talk to anyone? Maybe I'm the problem.*

- *I should be able to take care of this on my own.*

- *What's normal for children of this age anyway?*

Understanding the Benefits of Evaluation

Here may be the single most important point when considering whether your child has ADHD: evaluation is nothing more than an attempt to gather information. It's a first step in problem solving, not a commitment to any particular outcome.

When you begin to understand the reasons for your child's behavior, it affects your child's experience whether or not he has ADHD. You need to sort out what may be typical development, what seems quirky but fine, and where your child needs additional support. Whatever the situation, the earlier you and your child start cultivating new skills and habits, the easier things will be.

Too often, decisions around whether to evaluate and how to treat become entangled. Sometimes parents avoid evaluation because they fear an ADHD label. Yet most advice regarding child development is educational and useful, regardless of any diagnosis. And then, if your child is diagnosed with ADHD, it helps you better understand his experience and allows for clearer plans moving forward.

When pursuing an evaluation, find a developmental pediatrician, psychiatrist, neurologist, or psychologist to guide you through the process. You can get recommendations from your child's pediatrician, a parent-teacher association, or a parent network, such as Children and Adults with Attention Deficit Disorder (CHADD) or ImpactADHD. If an evaluation doesn't find ADHD or some other developmental condition—that's great news! And even then, there's a lot you can do to make things easier for you and your child.

Attention Doesn't Half Describe It: Defining ADHD

Attention deficit/hyperactivity disorder is a developmental condition characterized by inattention, hyperactivity, impulsiveness, and numerous issues related to self-management. For a diagnosis of ADHD, the symptoms must significantly differ from typical behavior of same-age peers and cause impairment somewhere in life. ADHD is not a behavioral disorder; it's a disorder of child development.

ADHD now describes what was once called ADD. The subtypes are categorized by predominant symptoms: inattention, hyperactivity/impulsiveness, or both. Many kids with ADHD primarily struggle with more hidden, internal symptoms. In spite of the fact that "hyperactivity" remains in the name, children can have ADHD without any sign of overactivity.

Exercise: Accentuating the Positive

Children's well-being and resilience depends on adults emphasizing their strengths. Some, hopefully, are obvious: playfulness, humor, kindness, warmth, imagination. Yet sometimes accentuating the positive might mean finding the silver lining in more difficult traits. For example, a stubborn child can be a challenge, but as he matures and you redirect his difficult behaviors, his tenacity and ability to persevere can become useful.

Shortly, you'll begin to address whatever worries you most about your child. But for this exercise, simply jot down your child's strengths. Then you can refer to this list as often as needed to help you keep the big picture in mind while you move forward and seek answers about your child's ADHD.

My child's strengths: _____

_____

_____

_____

_____

What It Means to Have ADHD

ADHD symptoms have been described both in pop culture and medical literature for well over a century. Consider this German nursery rhyme from the 1800s (Hoffman 2004):

"Let me see if Philip can

Be a little gentleman;

Let me see if he is able

To sit still for once at table":

Thus Papa bade Phil behave;

And Mamma looked very grave.

But fidgety Phil,

He won't sit still;

He wriggles

And giggles,

And then, I declare

Swings backwards and forwards

And tilts up his chair...

Medical discussion of ADHD is nearly as old, though until recently it used terms other than ADHD. So although understanding of ADHD has advanced leaps and bounds over the last several decades, the condition itself has been recognized for a long, long time.

Our overly fast-paced modern world creates so many distractions that people sometimes assume it's the root cause of attention disorders, yet ADHD is a specific medical condition. Genetic studies, brain imaging, and various biological risk factors (such as fetal alcohol syndrome) clearly define a disorder in which people struggle in a particular area of brain development for reasons entirely unrelated to their environment (Barkley 2006).

Broadly speaking, in ADHD, areas of the brain responsible for a wide-ranging group of self-management skills are underactive. Chronic issues with forgetfulness, time management, getting off task, not listening, and getting overly emotional when frustrated all reflect shortfalls in specific cognitive abilities. Just as some people can draw, shoot a basketball, or pick up playing an instrument more easily than others, skills such as planning, remembering, and paying attention are driven by genetics.

ADHD is typically characterized as a set of neurologically based symptoms falling into two broad categories: inattention and hyperactivity/impulsiveness (American Psychiatric Association 2013).

Inattention

- Often fails to give close attention to details or makes careless mistakes

- Often has trouble holding attention on tasks or play

- Often does not seem to listen when spoken to directly

- Often does not follow through on instructions and fails to finish schoolwork, chores, or work

- Often has trouble organizing tasks and activities

- Often avoids, dislikes, or is reluctant to do tasks that require mental effort over a long period of time (such as schoolwork or homework)

- Often loses things necessary for tasks and activities (school materials, pencils, books, tools, wallets, keys, paperwork, eyeglasses, cell phones, and so on)

- Is often easily distracted

- Is often forgetful in daily activities

Hyperactivity/Impulsiveness

- Often fidgets with or taps hands or feet, or squirms in seat

- Often leaves seat in situations when remaining seated is expected

- Often runs about or climbs in situations where it is inappropriate (in adolescents or adults, this symptom may be limited to feeling restless)

- Often unable to play or take part in leisure activities quietly

- Is often on the go, acting as if driven by a motor

- Often talks excessively

- Often blurts out an answer before a question has been completed

- Often has trouble waiting his or her turn

- Often interrupts or intrudes on others (such as butting in on conversations or games)

As you can probably see, many of these symptoms can be part of typical development. In the absence of demonstrable and prolonged impact, they basically represent nothing more than personality traits, some of which will change with age. In other words, a distractible or impulsive child who's doing fine in all areas of life can't have ADHD. And, as previously noted, ADHD can't be diagnosed unless the symptoms observed actually interfere with the child's life.

Celebrating differences and variety is, to fall back on a cliché, the spice of life. And, of course, young kids are often active, impulsive, and distractible. But when children chronically, though unintentionally, disrupt their own well-being, parents need to do something about it. If ADHD (or anything else) undermines a child's success, whether in the realm of play, learning, relationships, self-esteem, or any other part of life, we need to sort out why.

Some Key Facts About ADHD

- The genetics of ADHD are almost as strong as for height. Tall people tend to have tall children, regardless of who raises them. People with ADHD tend to have children with ADHD, regardless of who raises them (Biederman et al. 1995).

- An identical twin (even when living in another home) has as high as an 80 percent chance of having ADHD if the other twin has it. The risk for fraternal twins is near 30 percent (Gilger, Pennington, and DeFries 1992).

- If an immediate family member has ADHD, a child's risk is three to five times that of the general population (Barkley 2006).

- The rate of ADHD is similar around the world, affecting around 5 percent of children (Polanczyk et al. 2007).

- People with ADHD have consistently been shown to have smaller, less-active frontal lobes (along with other related areas of the brain) than other individuals (Dickstein et al. 2006). This is not a measure of intelligence. Instead, it relates to self-management skills (specifically, executive function, the topic of chapter 2).

Evaluating for ADHD or Ruling It Out

Diagnosing ADHD is a time-intensive process not based on any one test or source of information. Here's the short—but complete—list of what it takes for a professional to diagnose ADHD, followed by a longer description of each item:

- Documenting symptoms in different settings and across time

- Making certain nothing is mimicking ADHD or occurring along with it

- Determining where impairment is occurring in life

Documenting Symptoms in Different Settings and Across Time

In spite of near-conclusive brain research, and dissatisfying as it may feel, there is no gold standard for identifying ADHD. It is diagnosed by trying to prove that signs are present, ongoing, and undermining life. That starts with seeking possible symptoms of inattention or hyperactivity/impulsiveness in more than one setting (home, school, or elsewhere).

ADHD symptoms vary based on environmental demands, so different people may describe different patterns. For example, a teacher may report intense academic impairment in a child who has little trouble at home, or a parent may have concerns that teachers don't yet see. ADHD symptoms may also subtly affect other parts of a child's life, such as after-school activities, time with peers, or in managing logistics on his own. In fact, as discussed in chapter 2, the name itself—attention deficit/hyperactivity disorder—barely scratches the surface of its common manifestations.

The textbook approach to diagnosis emphasizes behavioral checklists that document common ADHD symptoms. Valid childhood measures include the Conners Parent and Teacher Rating Scales (Conners 1998), Vanderbilt Assessment Scales (Wolraich et al. 2003), SNAP Rating Scale (Atkins, Pelham, and Licht 1985), and Brown ADD Scales (T. E. Brown 1996), along with several others. All of these forms should be interpreted only in consultation with a professional; use them to gather your thoughts, but not to make a diagnosis (or rule one out) on your own.

The real-world experience of a child trumps any score on a questionnaire. Screening forms are considered reliable if they have near 80 percent accuracy, so about one in five may come back inaccurate. For example, they often fail to identify ADHD in bright, well-behaved students who have internal symptoms (daydreaming, forgetfulness, and so on) that fall beneath the radar in a busy home or classroom. Far more important than any particular test score is a clear understanding of an individual's overall life situation.

Professional evaluation involves getting to know a child and his parents both directly and through information gleaned from a variety of sources. Even direct observation has its limits, since in a quiet, one-on-one setting (like a professional's office), symptoms may not show up. A methodical clinician will integrate detailed medical and developmental history, school records and educational testing, therapist feedback, and any other available information to generate a larger view of the situation.

Keeping a Child's Age in Mind

To sort out a potential diagnosis, your child's development must be compared to same-age peers. Expectations for kindergarteners differ from those for fifth-graders, and expectations for kids in high school differ from those for young adults in college.

You may be surprised to know that ADHD diagnosis is possible even in preschoolers. A huge range of typical development exists in this age group, and a short attention span and high activity level are normal. However, further evaluation is warranted if a child is so active or poorly focused that he can't socialize, is a danger to himself, or can't sustain age-appropriate play.

That said, until age-expected demands escalate, milder and more internal symptoms (such as disorganization and distractibility) may not be apparent. ADHD may not overtly impact an individual's life until high school, college, or even later. So while the aim is to confirm symptoms in early childhood, that isn't always possible.

Another crucial aspect of evaluation is making sure demands on a child are appropriate for his age. In a world with increasingly rigorous academic requirements for increasingly younger children, the risk of misdiagnosis or overdiagnosis seems to be growing. Given the new emphasis on early academics and testing, typical young children may struggle to focus and perform in the classroom (Morrow et al. 2012; Hinshaw and Scheffler 2014). They also may become stressed and anxious about school.

It's imperative to separate policy-level concerns (too many children diagnosed in a community) with the needs of an individual who potentially has ADHD. The fact that misdiagnosis is possible doesn't mean much for someone who really has ADHD. Comprehensive evaluations consider "typical development" as one of many possibilities for a child.

Making Sure Nothing Is Mimicking ADHD or Occurring Along with It

The next aspect of evaluation is considering what else might be going on. Not everyone who has a hard time paying attention, socializing, or handling behavioral issues has ADHD. Here are some of the more common problems that may mimic ADHD:

- **Developmental disorders:** developmental delays (in language, motor, social, or other skills), cognitive impairments, autistic spectrum disorders, or learning disabilities

- **Mental health conditions:** anxiety, obsessive-compulsive disorder, depression, bipolar disorder, traumatic environments, or neglect

- **Physical conditions:** sleep apnea and other sleep disorders, thyroid disease, iron deficiency, or absence seizures (staring spells)

Screening for these other conditions is often straightforward, with other specific evidence pointing to the alternative diagnosis. ADHD-like symptoms are only very rarely caused by another medical or psychological condition without some evidence of this other condition being present. If a child has thyroid disease, he'll have medical symptoms; with autism, he'll have significant social, communication, and play delays; with an anxiety disorder, he'll have symptoms of anxiety; and so on.

That said, nearly two-thirds of people with ADHD have a second condition (MTA Cooperative Group 1999). Any initial evaluation must consider this possibility, especially because these coexisting conditions can be quite disruptive. The conditions that commonly co-occur with ADHD parallel the list of conditions that mimic it, making a knowledgeable professional crucial to the process of evaluation.

Here's an example: ADHD is a disorder that impairs life management, so it inherently causes a lot of anxiety. On the other hand, anxiety itself can make it very hard to learn and pay attention. Further, about one-third of people with ADHD also have an anxiety disorder. Whoever is evaluating your child must consider all these possibilities from the start.

Finally, bear in mind that a diagnosis of ADHD is a judgment call. If someone believed to have ADHD doesn't make progress despite a seemingly comprehensive intervention, the diagnosis itself should be reconsidered. However, it's equally important to consider whether a co-occurring condition was missed or whether an alternative intervention might be more effective.

Q&A

Q: I was all over the place when I was a child, and I didn't do so well in school. Now I'm doing great. How come that was fine then, but now we call it ADHD?

A: Seeing your own experience reflected in your child makes sense, given that the genetics of ADHD are strong. Sometimes that even leads to a delay in seeking help. But having impairment is necessary for an ADHD diagnosis, so if your life was totally fine during childhood, you didn't actually meet this criterion. Maybe your child's life is more impacted by it. On the other hand, maybe you struggled in some way and can help your child avoid that.

Determining Whether Impairment Is Occurring

Life impairments due to ADHD can be huge, such as major behavioral outbursts or an academic crisis. They can also be less dramatic but still important to consider, such as undermined relationships, low self-esteem, or heightened stress and anxiety.

Stereotyping ADHD as a disorder of misbehavior (active and impulsive) or school failure (daydreaming and disorganized) misses the point. As discussed in chapter 2, many children show more subtle patterns of ADHD-related impairment, especially as they get older. These children meet the criteria for diagnosis even if they're well behaved or succeeding in school.

Exercise: Assessing the Impacts of ADHD

These are some common real-life challenges linked to ADHD—outcomes stemming from the symptoms listed earlier in this chapter. Check off any that apply to your child so you can discuss them during the evaluation process:

- ☐ Difficulty sustaining or transitioning attention

- ☐ Becoming hyperfocused on enjoyable activities to the exclusion of anything else

- ☐ Fidgeting, hyperactivity, and impulsiveness

- ☐ Disorganization, forgetfulness, and carelessness

- ☐ Procrastination or other difficulties with time management

- ☐ Trouble remembering routines and following instructions

- ☐ Inconsistencies in behavior or academic performance

- ☐ Social and communication difficulties

- ☐ Sleep problems

- ☐ Overeating, eating disorders, or being overweight

- ☐ Struggling with reading, writing, or math

- ☐ Difficulties processing auditory information—not always seeming to hear or understand what others say

- ☐ Poor coordination or spatial awareness

- ☐ Frequent injuries or accidents due to distractibility, impulsiveness, or other aspects of self-management

- ☐ Substance abuse and smoking

Testing vs. Clinical Judgment

As mentioned, currently there isn't a single test for diagnosing ADHD. As our understanding of its impact on brain development grows, so does the possibility of definite measures to assess it. For now, as with many other medical disorders, accurate diagnosis relies mostly on professional judgment. Even neuropsychological testing, which includes various standardized measures of cognition, falls short in the real world. While often quite valuable, it may miss ADHD-related impairments that manifest in the classroom, at home, or during play.

You may have heard claims about more concrete-sounding measures of brain function. For example, computer tests of attention or tests that measure electrical activity in the brain offer data that can contribute to an evaluation. While the idea of concrete tests for ADHD may feel comforting, they are not yet adequate for identifying ADHD. Rating scales more accurately measure a person's actual experience, and clinical acumen trumps both.

The Role of Mindfulness

When parents are less stressed, more focused, more responsive, and more cognitively flexible in the face of challenges, their children clearly benefit. When they are less reflexively judgmental of themselves and others, that perspective changes how they relate to the world—and to ADHD itself. Mindfulness doesn't cure anything on its own, but it does influence ADHD by building traits that support the well-being of both parents and their children.

In her book *A Still Quiet Place*, physician Amy Saltzman defines mindfulness as "paying attention here and now, with kindness and curiosity, and then choosing your behavior" (Saltzman 2014, 9). While perfect as a description of what mindfulness is, that statement does not necessarily reveal to everyone mindfulness's tangible, day-to-day value. "Mindfulness" is a word used in an effort to translate an experience—something commonsense and accessible, but not easy to summarize in one sentence.

Shortly, this chapter turns to ways to practice and build mindfulness. But first, let's take a closer look at what mindfulness is—and what it isn't.

Mindfulness as a Skill Set

Stress frequently results when real life doesn't fit our idea of what should be. This might mean something as huge as *I imagined I'd be in a happy marriage forever, but now I'm getting divorced* or as mundane as *I had my heart set on a cheeseburger, but they're out of cheese.* When we're recently back from vacation, we may feel particularly magnanimous, accept our disappointment (at least with the cheeseburger), and move forward. But after an awful night's sleep and a fight with the boss, the no-cheese experience causes a meltdown. A lot of the time, if not all the time, our perspective matters when we face stressful situations.

Paying full attention to our immediate experience means focusing not just on external factors (*no cheese*) but our internal chatter (*This kind of thing always happens to me, What idiot failed to order cheese at a burger joint*). We can't expect to be happy in every situation, but we increase our suffering when we fuel our mental fires with self-recrimination (*I shouldn't make such a big deal over a piece of cheese*), rumination (*If I was a vegetarian this wouldn't happen to me*), prognosticating (*Nothing ever changes*), or other mental tinder.

Mindfulness is well captured by the familiar Serenity Prayer, without the God reference: "May I develop the ability to change the things I can, to accept the things I cannot, and the wisdom to see the difference." With mindfulness, we acknowledge the reality of the moment, however we may feel, without excessive wrestling, while proactively moving forward when we're able. Equanimity and a sense of peace and ease often follow.

So then, here's another way of understanding mindfulness: it's the ability to live more fully aware of what's transpiring around us and in our minds. Through that awareness, we become more familiar with our ongoing mental habits, increasing our ability to pick and choose (without expecting total success) which to continue and which to step back from at any moment.

We also build a general trait of responsiveness rather than reactivity. We create a little more space between our experience (*no cheese*) and whatever we elect to do next. Or maybe we allow ourselves to do or say nothing at all, letting go of rumination, planning, or a compulsion to fix everything: *I'm disappointed but don't have time to go elsewhere. What else can I order?*

Putting our existence under a microscope isn't the goal. Instead, we balance a more gentle focus with a measure of acceptance. We recognize our cognitive tendencies without self-criticism. We cultivate a sense of compassion for ourselves and others and recognize that once we pause and pay attention, we may notice that, in our own way, each of us tries to find some peace and happiness in life, even when we appear to be making a mess of it.

Common Confusion Around Mindfulness

There are often misperceptions about the relationship between mindfulness and meditation: Are they the same? Do you have to practice meditation to be mindful? And does mindfulness mean sitting quietly for hours on end and pretending to be happy about it?

Mindfulness meditation is a specific type of mental discipline designed to break a universal pattern: We all tend to live life distractedly, not quite paying attention to what's going on. We're on autopilot, relying on habitual and often reactive behaviors. Practicing mindfulness meditation, conversely, builds our capacity to focus more fully on life as it is, for better or worse, without escapism or striving for some kind of bliss. Not only *can* you meditate if you have a busy mind, it's *expected* that your mind will be busy.

Mindfulness, on the other hand, refers to a bigger package: a particular set of cognitive skills that can help you manage your life. Mindfulness doesn't require meditation, but meditation is a useful way to develop mindfulness. They are related but not identical.

Mindfulness in the West

Mindfulness isn't a spiritual practice unless you want it to be. Over the last several decades, scientist Jon Kabat-Zinn and many others have popularized centuries-old Buddhist concepts, without their religious context, in the secular West. Whether you're a business leader in Chicago, an inner-city kid from Baltimore, or a hermit on a Tibetan mountaintop, mindfulness will help you build skills and perspectives that cultivate a larger sense of equilibrium around basic facts of life—in particular, that everything is always changing, nothing stands still, and uncertainty rules.

Mindfulness classes often offer stress reduction, but they never promise to eliminate stress. Stress is going to continue no matter what you do. You'll still experience the highs and lows of life whether you practice mindfulness or not. And though your stress level could improve (as research suggests it often does), for some people mindfulness doesn't immediately alter anything. The practice isn't a cure-all or a quick fix. And it isn't specifically about stress, but holds a larger intent of building overall resilience and well-being.

In reality, mindfulness is a lifelong training. If you stick with it, even when practice is difficult and not much seems to happen, you will experience changes. Mindfulness is analogous to long-term physical training, rather than an acute intervention such as knee surgery or a dose of antibiotics.

Mindfulness for a Healthy Brain

You probably don't exercise because you want stronger lungs, legs, or arms specifically; you want your body as a whole to stay in shape. Likewise, the intent of mindfulness practice isn't a single specific improvement, like better focus, less stress, or less reactivity. Rather, you support a general state of mental well-being through ongoing effort. And that improves life not just for you, but for your family and anyone else who deals with you regularly.

As a pediatrician trained in Western medicine, the science of mindfulness matters a lot to me. Studies show that practicing mindfulness results in concrete physical changes in the brain (for example, Lazar et al. 2005; Leung et al. 2013), including ones related to focus and emotion regulation (Desbordes et al. 2012). Hundreds of other studies reveal that mindfulness offers numerous physical and psychological benefits, for everything from immune function and chronic pain to anxiety and depression (Davidson et al. 2003; Goyal et al. 2014). The brain is malleable, responding to our experience and reinforcing whatever we mentally practice with measurable physical growth throughout our entire lives. So if it clicks for you, feel free to define mindfulness as cognitive fitness training.

As you work your way through this book, then, remember that "mindfulness" is just a word—one that's less than perfect at encapsulating everything it covers. The concepts behind mindfulness are what matter. Try them as you read this book and find out for yourself.

Practice: Mindful Eating

As much as any activity, eating captures the concept of living on autopilot. Even with our favorite foods, most of us hardly notice the taste after the first few bites. We decide when, where, and how to eat based mostly on when, where, and how we've always eaten before—even when we know better.

When we don't devote attention to eating, we enjoy it less and are less healthy about it. We eat not only when we're hungry, but also because we're upset or just see an appealing dessert. We eat quickly and miss the slow-moving "I'm full" signal from the stomach. Recognizing these patterns as habit (and therefore not as permanent as they may seem) is a first step to altering them.

Below are instructions for a formal mindful eating practice—a common initial practice in mindfulness programs (for example, Kabat-Zinn 1991). Select any food, ideally something you can hold in your hand. Imagine you have no idea if it's edible or dangerous—as if you're encountering it for the first time. Take time with the process below, exploring each sensation along with whatever thoughts and emotions you notice.

Begin with vision: What does the object look like? What colors are present? What does light do when it hits the surface or when you move the object around? What else do you see?

What does the object feel like? Does it have any weight? What changes as you move it around?

Does it have an aroma?

Does it make a noise when you move it around?

Pause for a moment and notice: Where have your thoughts gone? Are you feeling anything in particular? Are you bored, restless, or feeling awkward? Are you excited about trying this out, or doubtful that it could be helpful for you? Recognize those experiences too, then return your attention to this exercise.

Choose the moment when you'd like to place the object between your teeth. And then pause before proceeding.

Now put the object in your mouth, adding the sense of taste. Observe taste, as well as what changes with each of your other senses.

Chew just once, then pause. Review the details of your experience, including the five senses, your thoughts, and your feelings. When your attention strays, return to the practice again.

Continue chewing with the same intention. As you chew, does the taste, smell, or physical sensation change?

Before swallowing, pause and decide when it's time to do so. Then swallow. Can you feel the food moving all the way down to your stomach?

Taking the same approach to each bite, continue until you decide the practice is done.

You always have the option of paying attention to eating. Practice putting down your utensil between bites and consciously deciding when to take another one. Pause before making food choices—not to give yourself a hard time, but to be aware that you actually have a choice. Likewise, when preparing food pay full attention to the process, allowing your mind to focus on the activity instead of being caught up in worries, plans, or other thoughts. In this way, you can use an everyday experience to build your capacity for giving life the full attention it deserves.

A Few Tidbits About Eating Mindfully

- Don't have time for eating an entire meal in this way? Just take the first few bites with awareness.

- Use a snack, coffee break, or something similar anytime during the day to set aside some time for yourself and focus on what you're eating or drinking; it doesn't even have to be quiet around you. When you get caught up in distracting thoughts or difficult emotions, bring attention back to your immediate experience: *For all of the noise and chaos going on around me, here I am, sitting with a hot cup of coffee.*

- Use smaller plates or bowls, encouraging a pause between refills.

- Turn off the television and smartphones during meals to decrease distracted eating and ensure you're giving direct attention to your kids.

Start Taking a Mindful Approach to ADHD Today

If the word "mindfulness" seems strange, drop the word. You'll still benefit from taking a few moments for self-care, paying attention to your experience, and building cognitive traits such as compassion, responsiveness (rather than reactivity), and flexibility in problem solving. Change is not only possible but inevitable, and we each have the potential to influence whatever happens next in our lives. Use any words that work for you to describe your aims.

To manage your child's ADHD, you need to develop an objective view of his abilities and strengths, a far more subtle task than it may seem on the surface. Only then can you engage in detailed planning to build your child's skills and create compensatory strategies to help him overcome ADHD. You need to encourage appropriate behavior and hard work but remain aware that your child is doing his best at any given moment, even when ADHD gets in the way.

Action Plan: Getting Started on a Mindful Path to Managing ADHD

If you haven't yet determined whether your child has ADHD, use the checklist below to coordinate an evaluation. If your child has already received a diagnosis, use the checklist to begin your mindfulness practice. Start your family on this new path right now, today, by taking these next steps toward change.

- [ ] Find accurate resources to educate yourself about ADHD:

    - [ ] Start with this book, which is entirely evidence-based.

    - [ ] Visit websites produced by a credible ADHD parent network (such as CHADD or ImpactADHD).

    - [ ] Review the ADHD information at the website of the American Academy of Pediatrics (http://www.healthychildren.org, under the "Health Issues" tab).

- [ ] Contact a specialist who understands ADHD and conducts evaluations. This will typically be a developmental pediatrician, psychologist, neurologist, or psychiatrist. To locate a specialist, consider getting a referral from one of the following sources:

    - [ ] Use the referral feature at the websites of ADHD support networks.

    - [ ] Ask your child's pediatrician for a referral.

    - [ ] Inquire at local groups such as parent-teacher organizations.

- [ ] Once you've located a specialist, confirm that the evaluation will involve a review of your child's history, gathering of new information, and screening for co-occurring conditions.

    - [ ] Schedule an appointment. Write the appointment time here:

    _____

- [ ] Gather needed information:

    - [ ] Collect your child's report cards or interim reports if available.

☐ Request copies of psychoeducational testing completed in school or elsewhere.

☐ Collect any completed ADHD rating scales and request updated ones from your child's pediatrician.

☐ Begin practicing mindfulness:

☐ Eat one meal or snack daily following the guidelines for mindful eating.

☐ Set up some reminders right now:

☐ Post this checklist where you'll see it every day, or create a whiteboard dedicated to your plans for managing your child's ADHD.

☐ Use your smartphone or calendar to set up reminders to complete the tasks on this list.

☐ When you forget to work on your plan for a day (or several days), return to it without giving yourself a hard time. It happens to everyone!

☐ Continue using similar reminders for the action plan at the end of each chapter.

Chapter 2

Looking at ADHD Through the Lens of Executive Function

Read this chapter to...

- Understand how executive function, a set of mental skills, serves as the "brain manager" in helping coordinate thoughts and actions

- Understand ADHD as a developmental disorder of executive function

- Manage stress to support yourself and your family while augmenting your child's ADHD care

Nothing quite captures the sense that the world is inherently changing and uncertain more than having children. We have hopes and ambitions about what their childhood will look like. We have hopes and ambitions about how we'll perform in the grand role of Parent. And then life shows up, and most of that tends to go out the window.

Maybe your imagined baseball player loves geology and shuns athletics, or your imagined scientist does poorly in math but great in art. You may have a handle on how to talk to a fifth-grader, but then time passes and you find yourself stymied by a moody teenager. Your own tranquil temperament may sometimes explode in a fiery blast of frustration. And those examples don't even begin to get into the far more intense and serious circumstances all parents face at some point.

How we deal with the unexpected affects our family life. When stressed, we're more likely to be reactive and fall back on entrenched habits, rather than making proactive, skilled decisions. And as it turns out, one of the best predictors of a child's stress is her parents' stress level. So if you feel resilient and settled, that supports your entire family.

Managing ADHD requires persistence, flexible problem solving, and endless compassion. By cultivating those traits in yourself through mindfulness practice, you improve your child's life. Aiming to see life as it is, you can better recognize the nuances of ADHD in order to identify your child's needs. To do that, you must see past the traditional definition of ADHD as a disorder of attention and instead understand it in relation to a much larger set of cognitive skills called executive function.

ADHD and Brain Management Central

What does "executive function" mean? Just as a business requires someone to synchronize the activity of its employees, the brain must coordinate our experience. One part of the brain, the frontal lobes, integrates what we know with what we experience and what we do. Executive function encompasses the underlying set of management skills required to accomplish this. It also relates to vital developmental tasks such as developing self-regulation and emotional resilience. When a child has ADHD, her executive function doesn't work efficiently, and this has impacts far and wide.

As mentioned in chapter 1, chronic procrastination and disorganization lie at the core of ADHD, as does poor sleep. Unhealthy eating habits and being overweight are common. ADHD has been linked to more numerous emergency room visits for injuries and, for teens, more car accidents. Executive function also supports communication and social engagement, and children with ADHD may have difficulties with both.

ADHD is like an iceberg (Dendy and Zeigler 2003). Above the water, obvious at first glance, are symptoms such as poor focus and impulsivity. Hidden below the surface are the many other impairments caused by impaired executive function—in other words, an inefficient, off-task brain manager.

How Executive Function Develops

Robust executive function has been linked to everything from financial and marital success to academic progress and physical health. Preschoolers with stronger executive function skills appear more likely to succeed academically all the way through college. One study even linked preschool executive function with later measures of health, wealth, and criminality (Moffitt et al. 2011). Of course, not every child who struggles with executive function experiences lifelong difficulty; these are just trends across groups.

As with developing language, motor, and social abilities, there is a typical path to mature executive function. In fact, recent research shows that these skills continue to mature until people are almost thirty years old, probably explaining, at least in part, why up to half of children outgrow ADHD (Hinshaw and Scheffler 2014).

As executive function develops, toddlers learn impulse control, and preschoolers gain the capacity to take others' perspective. By school age, classroom learning relies on skills related to executive function (such as memory, organization, and planning), as well as improved attention. The capacity to defer gratification continues to grow all the way into adulthood.

Understanding this trajectory helps us understand children. You wouldn't expect a four-year-old to organize getting out the door. A preschooler, given time, could probably list the steps: get dressed, have breakfast, brush teeth. But she can't coordinate these activities, remember the details, or stay on task as long as needed, whereas most teenagers can manage this on their own. Much of what changes is related to executive function.

Teens Are Teens, Not Adults

Most teenagers couldn't run a household while holding a job. But by their twenties, most live independently and some have families. What's changed?

Puberty includes a burst of development in areas of the brain linked to executive function. Before adulthood, planning, management skills, long-term thinking, and impulse control aren't fully present.

We all probably know a precocious teen capable of incredible foresight and life management, but most teens don't have adult-level skills. Without mature executive function, no one can be expected to act like a full-fledged grown-up.

Adolescents strive for independence and need opportunities to try things out on their own, but they lack mature executive function. They may not see the potential implications of getting a tattoo on their face or texting a risqué photo to a new love interest. While it's important to encourage their exploration and growth, adult guidance must continue until they prove responsible. And if they have ADHD, that might be later than typical among their peers.

Practice: Letting Go of Assumptions

When what we expect contradicts what we find, it heightens our discomfort. It also affects how we approach a problem. If you expect a four-year-old to complete her bedtime routine without any adult help, you're going to be stressed. Most four-year-olds can't accomplish that. If you believe a four-year-old will require a lot of adult guidance in that task, you'll feel better about it, even though you're just as busy. But what about a seven-year-old with ADHD who has the self-regulatory skills of a four-year-old? Assumptions about what should happen and why it happened affect your experience and that of your child.

Take a moment to imagine a challenging situation involving your child. Choose something only moderately irritating to begin with. As you picture the scenario in more detail, notice the stress that arises even when you just think about it. Observe the causes you attribute the problem to: lack of effort, willfulness, laziness, or whatever seems apparent on the surface.

Next, take a few breaths and then mentally take a step back, adopting the theoretical view that ADHD alone underlies the issue. Might your child's intentions be different than they seem? Would your attitude toward the situation shift if you saw this problematic behavior as the result of a developmental delay in particular skills? For any challenge or decision that arises in parenting, there can be value to pausing in this way, checking in with your assumptions, and then readjusting if needed.

Practical Parenting: Seeing Children Through the Lens of Executive Function

Executive function isn't an esoteric, academic topic. Understanding it helps us to meet children where they are developmentally. Kids with ADHD don't want to mess up any more than children with language delays intend to have difficulty with conversation.

All children would thrive if only they knew how. Not many kids intentionally fail to hand in a paper they finished the night before or go out of their way to alienate friends. While acknowledging how exhausting and frustrating ADHD is for parents and teachers, we need to seek the reasons for problem behaviors and take practical steps based on what we find.

The following framework, modeled after an outline created by ADHD expert Thomas E. Brown (2006), defines executive function based on six related skill groups:

- Attention management

- Action management

- Task management

- Information management

- Emotion management

- Effort management

As you'll see, understanding ADHD in this way allows you to better identify how you can support your child. No child with ADHD has full deficits across all these areas, but almost all have differences in some. Breaking down any task or behavior in light of executive function allows for more targeted solutions, whether at home, at school, or elsewhere.

Attention Management

ADHD doesn't cause an inability to pay attention; rather, it creates difficulty with attention management as a whole. It leads to trouble focusing when demands rise, being overly focused when intensely engaged, and difficulty shifting attention. Here are a few common situations that arise with ADHD:

- **Hyperfocusing on what seems fun and cognitively effortless.** People often assume that children with ADHD selectively choose to pay attention, getting distracted only when disinterested. In reality, they cannot (as opposed to will not) focus when mentally challenged. The ability to endlessly stick with video games or other enjoyable activities, even reading, doesn't eliminate the possibility of ADHD when a child has difficulty focusing otherwise.

- **Being challenged by distracting environments.** Proper focus allows attention to remain with one element within a crowd, such as one voice among many. In busy situations, kids with ADHD often lose details of what's said and may shut down, feel overwhelmed, or act out.

- **Having difficulty transitioning away from activities.** If you make a request while a child with ADHD is engrossed with something else, it won't register. This trait often leads to a perception of bad behavior: *I spoke and was ignored.* As is often the case with ADHD, the solution lies in an adult's choices. There's no point speaking until you have your child's full attention.

Action Management

Action management is the ability to monitor your own physical activity and behavior. Delays in this aspect of executive function lead to symptoms such as fidgeting, hyperactivity, and impulsiveness. Problems with action management also mean it takes longer to learn from mistakes, as doing so requires awareness of the details and consequences of actions. This helps explain why behavioral change is slower for children with ADHD. Self-monitoring of social behavior is also an aspect of action management.

In addition, deficiencies in this aspect of executive function often cause delayed development of motor abilities, poor coordination, or trouble with handwriting. Children with ADHD may also meet criteria for developmental coordination disorder, in which case occupational therapy can help them catch up.

Task Management

Task management calls on various core executive function abilities, including organizing, planning, prioritizing, and monitoring time. If you're able to manage life easily and instinctually, it may seem unimaginable that your child doesn't have a sense of what's happening today or this week, or that she ignores projects until it's a last-minute crisis. Yet these skills lie on a developmental path directly affected by ADHD, and as children get older, task management (not attention) often becomes the core issue. Unlike some ADHD-related difficulties, task management doesn't respond robustly to medication. Teaching your child organizational skills is the solution, as addressed in chapter 4.

Information Management

Working memory is the capacity to manage the voluminous information we encounter in the world and integrate it with what we know. Like RAM on a computer, the brain temporarily holds information when accessing it and organizing our ideas. These functions underlie skills in conversation, reading, and writing, and therefore directly affect classroom learning.

Working memory holds short-term information that isn't necessary to memorize, such as a string of requests. So if your send your child off to accomplish several things at once ("Run up to your room, change into your soccer clothes, and put your school clothes in the hamper"), the details scatter in the wind.

Losing track can look like misbehavior when you find your child playing instead of following through, but it actually reflects poor working memory, and perhaps distractibility. However, actual misbehavior can follow if your child scrambles to cover up. But if you give her a written list or a shorter list of verbal instructions, she might do just fine.

Emotion Management

Emotional reactivity is often an inherent part of ADHD. Kids with ADHD may be quick to anger, give up, or get frustrated or upset. This emotionality may come across as oppositional. Everyone gets annoyed at times, but those with ADHD may not have enough of an ability to rein in their emotions, causing them to react immediately when rattled.

This type of reactivity isn't the same as the random emotional volatility of a mood disorder. And while it may not be apparent on the surface, an outburst may be followed by regret or embarrassment. This can lead to excuses, more anger, or shutting down, escalating the behavioral stakes. This isn't a second condition tagging along with ADHD; it *is* ADHD.

Effort Management

Executive function underlies the ability to maintain effort until an activity is completed. Difficulties with sustained effort often get labeled as poor motivation. Your child may go upstairs to do homework, and thirty minutes later you find her reading a graphic novel. Because of difficulties with effort management she ran out of steam, but to you it may seem that she doesn't value her work.

Processing speed can also be a factor in effort management. The ability to work quickly and effectively may be impaired in some kids with ADHD. However, working more slowly is in no way a reflection of their intelligence.

For many kids with ADHD, external pressure may decrease productivity. Instead of the frontal lobes leaping into action, the mental gears lock up. Stress decreases cognitive efficiency, making it harder to solve problems and make choices. This undermines everything from getting out of the house on time to taking tests.

But Wait, There's More!

Understanding children with ADHD comes down to how it manifests in real life. Not all aspects of ADHD fit neatly into this executive function model, and many symptoms of ADHD stem from multiple aspects of executive function. Here are some other common patterns to look out for.

Delayed Ability to Learn Routines

Executive function skills are required to maintain routines. One impact of ADHD is a chronic struggle with day-to-day activities like getting out the door in the morning, homework, and healthy sleep, eating, and exercise habits (all addressed in later chapters). You may need to help your child manage these routines far longer than other kids would require.

Inconsistent Performance

Kids with ADHD often have a befuddling tendency to show particular skills sometimes, but not often enough. This leads to a perception that they just need to try harder: *If you can focus well on your video game or stay organized while trying to win a prize, why not all the time?*

Here's the catch: Their inconsistency *is* their ADHD. If they could succeed more often, they would. Strong executive function allows people to capitalize on their strengths. Without it, kids experience being on the ball some days, seemingly at random, along with far too many days when they aren't. Therefore, one measure of successful ADHD management is when a child seems at her personal best more consistently.

Social Immaturity

Children with ADHD often seem immature compared to their peers—because they are. Many traits that define maturity involve executive function skills, such as impulse control, forethought, planning, and perspective taking. Thankfully, children with ADHD can catch up when given appropriate support.

Apparent Lack of Motivation

The interrelationship between motivation and ADHD is complicated. Motivation depends on not just desire, but also neurological ability. With ADHD, the brain doesn't stay engaged long enough for follow-through.

ADHD also impairs the capacity to identify and maintain long-term objectives, which is, of course, another defining aspect of motivation. From the outside, this getting off task looks like low motivation. Of course, kids with ADHD may also become less motivated in the traditional sense. When they try and try and still don't succeed because of their ADHD, they may give up. The solution isn't to push them harder, but to provide support that facilitates their progress.

Impaired Time Management and Procrastination

People with ADHD often have difficulty with managing time. This manifests as a complex pattern with a variety of causes and effects:

- **Difficulty managing projects across time.** Long-term tasks may take longer than anticipated because of not seeing the steps required, creating a kind of procrastination by default. A child sets out to get a huge report done but doesn't consider trips to the library, outlining, and other intermediate steps. So although she aims to do well, she'll fall behind and be pressured in the end.

- **Challenges in planning due to difficulty estimating how much time tasks will take.** The same student might falsely predict how much time is needed for large tasks and therefore leave things to the last minute. *I'll watch the end of the movie tonight and write my paper before the bus tomorrow.* But if she doesn't finish the paper because it can't be done in thirty minutes, she wasn't really procrastinating—she just misread the situation.

- **Difficulty with prioritizing.** Organizing activities based on importance is a cognitive skill directly impacted by ADHD. For kids with ADHD, it's also complicated by difficulties with transitioning attention smoothly and tracking time accurately. Like many kids, your child may get home from school and feel tired or want to play for a while. But then hours may pass without her realizing it. She thinks she'll do her homework eventually, but then it gets late and she wonders where the evening went.

- **Developing a pattern around procrastination because it improves focus.** When under pressure to perform, some kids with ADHD actually experience better attention for a few hours. Whether consciously or unconsciously, these kids discover that procrastinating seems to help get them get things done by creating last-minute pressure. Unfortunately, procrastination leads to rushed, low-quality work, with little time for correction. It also takes a physical and emotional toll.

Q&A

Q: If a child has executive function problems, does that always mean ADHD?

A: ADHD is the most common condition related to impaired executive function. However, other challenges such as learning disabilities, autism, and various mental health conditions may impact it too. These other conditions can also co-occur with ADHD, muddling the discussion. But if a child has significant executive function issues, ADHD is probably part of the picture.

Another Hurdle: Not Getting to Task Completion

Any plan has three parts: First, we need to prepare. Second, we need to act. And third, we need to complete what we started. With ADHD, the last step chronically gets left out. A person gets partway through a task and then, without noticing, moves on to something else.

To complete homework, a child needs to write down assignments at school and bring books home. Once home, she needs to focus and complete the work. Finally, she needs to return materials to her backpack and remember to turn in her homework the next day.

You may have the experience that a trail follows your child throughout her day. Her toothbrush is on the back of the toilet, Legos are strewn on the floor, pajamas lie beneath the kitchen table, and various drawers are left half open after a failed search for a pen. The third part of any activity, completing what we start, involves putting things away, but for kids with ADHD that may happen seldom at best.

As is often the case, recognizing the pattern is the first step toward change. Your child may be in the middle of one activity yet already be mentally involved in the next. It can be helpful to document routines in writing: "Completing homework means placing it in its folder," "Every night after dinner, we clean up the playroom," and so on. Another technique is to directly build a new habit of pausing before transitions, as described in the next exercise. With support, practice, and patience, children can consistently complete what they set out to do.

Practice: Learning to STOP

One way of fostering the ability to complete tasks is to cultivate a habitual pause when transitioning between activities. Your child probably knows the last step in any activity—actually completing it—but her ADHD causes her to skip it. To counter this tendency, the STOP practice (Stahl and Goldstein 2010) creates an opportunity to "remember to remember" what happens last. Reinforcing a habitual pause before transitions or decisions builds a new habit that can be helpful for anyone. Practice this technique on your own for a while before teaching it to your child. That way you'll become familiar with it—including its benefits for you.

To create this pause, practice the STOP acronym below with each transition. It may take a while (perhaps weeks or even months), but this new habit can become instinct. To practice, simply notice moments of transition during your day: getting up from the dining table, leaving your desk, or shifting between activities. In those moments, follow these four steps:

S　=　Stop what you're doing.

T　=　Take a few breaths.

O　=　Observe what's going on, both internally and externally.

P　=　Proceed with intention, choosing what would be best to do next.

How does this approach help a child? It can look like this: *I'm done with homework, let's see, where's my baseball glove*, and, pausing, she returns her attention to the moment, notices her desk, and moves her books into her backpack. Post a stop sign on your child's bulletin board or to-do list to serve as a reminder. You can also post reminders, both for yourself and for your child, on the refrigerator or a mirror or calendar, or set up a reminder on a smartphone. It may not be on the first try or the tenth or even the twentieth, but eventually, a new habit encodes itself in the brain for you and your child.

ADHD and the Elephant in the Room

You may be familiar with the story of five blind men who on a walk encounter an elephant. One grasps the trunk and says, "I've found a snake." Another presses the side and declares, "We've come to a wall." One grabs a leg and says, "Not at all. It's a tree." The next touches its tail and says, "There's a rope." The last one feels a tusk and pronounces, "No, I think it's some kind of pipe."

Executive function problems can undermine almost any aspect of life, generating symptoms that may seem as diverse as snake, wall, tree, rope, or pipe. Yet no symptom of ADHD exists in isolation. Underneath ADHD's multifaceted presentation is a single elephant that explains countless childhood experiences. When we don't take the entirety of ADHD into consideration, interventions may be piecemeal and less effective.

You can waste a lot of time, energy, and money by focusing on parts of your child's ADHD instead of the whole picture. Sometimes new claims and new products are offered based on theories about child development, without any evidence that these approaches work, diverting families from interventions more likely to succeed. Lately, the term "processing disorder" has risen to the fore. Yet many issues labeled "processing disorders" are actually symptoms of ADHD:

- **Auditory processing.** Children with ADHD have a difficult time with complex auditory information. In a busy situation, such as a classroom with several people speaking, they can't handle the barrage of sound. If they're spoken to while doing something else, they'll miss details. Language and learning disabilities also affect auditory processing and may explain this symptom.

- **Visual processing and tracking.** Children with poor executive function may seem to have visual symptoms because their eyes jump around the page when they read, they miss words or word endings, or they lose their place. Even letter reversals (such as mistaking b for d), which are commonly linked to reading disabilities, don't occur because of anything visual.

- **Sensory processing.** Some children have actual sensory sensitivities, such as disliking touch or noise. However, this term also gets applied to often unrelated symptoms such as skin picking, anxiety, or elevated physical activity. An anxious child freaking out in a crowd could be sensitive to noise but probably is only scared. An active child doesn't "seek sensory input"; rather, she may be hyperactive because of the underactive frontal lobes associated with ADHD. Some sensory issues are real, but research hasn't yet established a "sensory integration disorder" separate from other diagnoses such as ADHD.

Identifying auditory, sensory, and visual concerns has value. Speech-language and occupational therapists have vital roles in ADHD care. True vision issues should be addressed. However, these interventions help most when they're part of an integrated approach. (If you'd like to read articles and policy statements about these common misperceptions, a downloadable document, "National Statements on Processing Disorders," is available at http://www.newharbinger.com/31793.)

Seeing the parts of the "ADHD elephant" as separate may feel overwhelming. Your child may have trouble with focus, poor reading comprehension skills, and difficulty with auditory processing. Trying to address each separately could be time-consuming, expensive, and exhausting. Recognizing a unifying condition reframes the situation: ADHD underlies all of it, and that's what should be addressed.

Exercise: Addressing Executive Function When Problem Solving

Different children with ADHD have different patterns of executive function deficits. To create an individualized, integrated plan, you need to observe your child, try things out, and readjust as needed. Seeing your child's ADHD through the lens of executive function difficulties will help you tailor your parenting to your child's strengths and adapt to her needs.

In this exercise, you'll explore how difficulties with executive function may be involved in one of your child's challenges. If you find this approach helpful, you may want to use it for other concerns. (A downloadable worksheet is available on the website associated with this book.)

Because this perspective may be new, let's start with an example.

Behavioral or academic concern: *My daughter never gets ready for school without constant reminders and bickering.*

Role of attention management: *She cannot (as opposed to will not) concentrate. She's distractible and easily gets off task.*

Role of action management: *She runs around excessively and impulsively pushes her sister.*

Role of task management: *She can't keep track of time or independently plan what she needs to accomplish.*

Role of information management: *She can't hold the list of what she needs to do in her mind, even though she knows what she must do.*

Role of emotion management: *She gets overly upset when redirected from play.*

Role of effort management: *She can't sustain attention to complete tasks such as getting dressed without going off and playing.*

Now it's your turn. Write down a behavioral challenge, then examine how each aspect of executive function might play a role. If need be, refer back to the descriptions earlier in this chapter to guide your understanding.

Behavioral or academic concern: _____

_____

Role of attention management: _____

_____

Role of action management: _____

_____

Role of task management: _____

_____

Role of information management: _____

_____

Role of emotion management: _____

_____

Role of effort management: _____

_____

A Mindful Approach to Stress

Stress, uncertainty, and being a parent all go hand in hand. This stress affects how you live, how you relate to others, and how effectively you manage your child's ADHD. Just as you'll benefit from seeing your child's challenges through the lens of executive function, it's helpful to understand how your own neurology may be affecting you—specifically, in your experience of stress.

Some amount of stress keeps us motivated and safe. When we feel threatened, our nervous system is wired to produce the physiological reactions known as the stress (or fight-or-flight) response, readying us to protect ourselves or flee from danger. We spring into action without thought—a good thing when dodging out of the way of an oncoming car. Our bodies pour energy toward muscles and away from the digestive system. Reflexes control our arms and legs, and rational thought stops. These reactions can be lifesaving—when we're in actual danger.

The problem is, our response to stress isn't subtle. The same physiological reactions arise after anything rattles us, including thoughts: *I'm late. I'm bad at this. They don't like me.* The cycle revs up the body and shuts down cognitive skills, since there's no time for thinking when we're in acute danger. The brain sends out signals that a crisis looms, but in most cases, these aren't life-threatening situations; there's no lion about to eat us.

Most often, stress starts with a perception, perhaps outside our conscious awareness, that something isn't as we think it should be. We're just running a little late or worried about our to-do list. Yet that same intense stress reaction occurs.

Nothing will ever completely eliminate stress. In fact, some amount of stress may even keep us motivated. However, our bodies aren't wired to withstand overly frequent or intense stress. And because excessive stress undermines both physical and mental health, it affects not just you, but the people around you. Among other things, it can make it hard for you to stay on top of your child's ADHD care.

One of the most exciting developments in neuroscience over the last decade is the discovery of neuroplasticity. The human brain rewires itself based on any behavior, or even thought, that we reinforce through repetition. When you work on increasing your focus or consciously adopt new habits, neurologic change follows. You can't erase genetics, but by adjusting how you live, you can change many traits that may otherwise seem ingrained.

You can elect to cultivate traits that will be helpful in managing whatever life brings your way. That typically starts with devoting more attention to your real-time experience and finding more space between what you observe and what you decide to do next. Setting aside even a few minutes daily for a mindfulness practice, such as the one that follows, will help you build this capacity.

Practice: Awareness of the Breath

This practice will help you guide your attention more often to the present, rather than being caught up in your mind. The sensation of breathing is often used only because your breath is with you all the time. The practice isn't about trying to change how you breathe; your breath simply provides a focus for your attention.

With mindfulness, the only intention is to attend to the moment as best you can. You aren't striving to transcend anything, get anywhere, or block out anything out. There's not even a goal of relaxation. That often happens, but you can't force yourself into feeling it.

You cannot be good or bad at meditation. You'll never fix unwavering attention on your breath. Some days meditation allows you a few moments of peace; other days your mind will remain busy. If you're distracted almost the entire time and still come back to one breath, that's perfect. And if you practice, you'll find yourself focusing more often on life with less effort.

Below, you'll find instructions for practicing focused awareness (audio download available).

Sit comfortably, finding a stable position you can maintain for a while, either on the floor or in a chair. If not using guided audio, set a timer to avoid clock-watching.

Close your eyes if you like, or leave them open and gaze downward toward the floor.

Draw attention to the physical sensation of breathing, perhaps noticing the always-present rising and falling of your abdomen or chest, or perhaps the air moving in and out through your nose or mouth. With each breath, bring attention to these sensations. If you like, mentally note, "Breathing in... Breathing out."

Many times over, you'll get distracted by thoughts or feelings. You may feel distracted more often than not. That's normal. There's no need to block or eliminate thinking or anything else. Without giving yourself a hard time or expecting anything different, when you discover that your attention has wandered, notice whatever has distracted you and then come back to the breath.

Practice pausing before making any physical adjustments, such as moving your body or scratching an itch. With intention, shift at a moment you choose, allowing space between what you experience and what you choose to do.

Let go of any sense of trying to make something happen. For these few minutes, create an opportunity to not plan or fix or whatever else is your habit. Exert enough effort to sustain this practice, but without causing yourself mental strain. Seek balance; if you find yourself mostly daydreaming and off in fantasy, devote a little extra effort to maintaining your focus.

Breathing in and breathing out, return your attention to the breath each time it wanders elsewhere.

Practice observing without needing to react. Just sit and pay attention. As hard as it is to maintain, that's all there is. Come back over and over again without judgment or expectation. It may seem simple, but it's never easy.

Informal Mindfulness Practice

Practices like the preceding one are generally considered to be formal practices, conducted at scheduled times and usually in a set location. You can also practice mindfulness informally during any activity, from folding the laundry to conversing with a coworker.

Practice: Informal Mindfulness in Day-to-Day Activities

Throughout the day, you can aim to be more mindful whenever you choose, electing to give full attention, as best you can, to anything you're doing. If you're playing catch in the backyard, attend as fully as possible just to that experience instead of throwing the ball while thinking of challenges you may face later, like getting your child through homework. If you're making dinner, focus on all the sensations involved in preparing the meal, rather than ruminating about your day. Not only will you be cultivating more focused attention within yourself, but you'll also create a momentary break when you guide your attention out of distracting or unsettling thoughts.

Action Plan: Bringing Increased Awareness to Your Child's ADHD

When you expand your understanding of how executive function influences your child's experience, your capacity to adapt and address her ADHD fundamentally changes. And as you begin to focus more awareness on your own immediate experience, your ability to more calmly and resolutely manage ADHD will improve as well. Creating an effective plan for managing your child's ADHD requires letting go of prior assumptions and observing what is, with curiosity and without judgment, a process supported by the practice of mindfulness.

☐ Observe your child's experience through the lens of executive function. Use the information in this chapter to reframe ADHD as a developmental delay requiring specific supports.

☐ If you find it helpful, come up with a simple statement for reminding yourself that an ADHD symptom is no one's fault, including your child's. Record your statement below, and then, when you feel exasperated, angry, or upset, repeat this statement to yourself:

_____

_____

☐ Dedicate time each day to doing an enjoyable activity with your child, choosing something that already happens in everyday life. As much as possible give your full attention to your child during this time together. Write the activity you've chosen here:

_____

☐ Practice the focused awareness meditation in this chapter or the eating meditation from chapter 1 daily. Consider tying this plan to something already consistent for you, like after you put your kids on the bus or at the start of your lunch break. Write your practice time here:

_____

☐ Use the STOP practice often and teach your child this skill. Post visual reminders to STOP wherever you and your child will see them often, such as on the fridge, your computer screen, or near your child's desk.

Chapter 3

Why Your Self-Care Matters for Your Child

Read this chapter to...

- Recognize both obvious and subtle effects of ADHD on families and relationships

- Address the unique impacts of ADHD on everyone in your family

- See how paying attention more fully, in real time, will benefit you and your family and help you manage your child's ADHD

L ife is here. Our attention usually isn't. While eating breakfast with our children, we may be mulling over an argument. While putting them on the bus, perhaps we're already mentally at the gym. At the gym, we may be dreading their homework. And while battling over homework, we're anticipating the next seven years of school. Doing one thing while attending to another, we're on autopilot, speaking and acting without genuine awareness.

When we're caught up in ruminating over the past or planning the future, the present moment passes unattended. We miss chances to talk or joke around with our kids. Or perhaps we're trying to focus on praise and reward as part of a new behavioral plan, but lost in distraction, we overlook something that actually went well.

Living on autopilot increases stress, turning mental brush fires into conflagrations. We lose the opportunity to consider our actions, assumptions, and countless thoughts, emotions, and memories, all of which can cause or increase stress. We can influence the future with planning, but the only moment in which we can actually do something concrete is the one right in front of us. Unfortunately, most of the time we're not paying a whole lot of attention to that moment at all.

As you'll continue to learn and experience, the simple act of paying attention with mindfulness has profound benefits. It's one of the best things you can do for your own self-care, and to enhance your ability to help your child with ADHD.

The Impact of ADHD on Parents

A child's ADHD has many underacknowledged, direct impacts on his parents. ADHD interventions often rely on parental consistency and responsiveness, including in conflict management. These qualities are often difficult for parents to sustain day in, day out when their child has ADHD.

Being a parent takes work, despite its many joys. You aim to manage both the difficult and the mundane with a measure of sanity, and to sustain your best effort. Even as you grasp how to manage a particular age, your child gets older, so you scramble to adjust again. It's a uniquely wondrous, gratifying, and not always easy experience.

In addition to educating yourself about your child's ADHD, it's important to understand how it affects you and how you can manage that impact. So for the sake of your child, let's take a quick look at some of the challenges you may face as a parent.

Parenting a child who's struggling is stressful. All parents want their children to be successful and content, however they picture that ideal. But by definition, children with ADHD are impaired in some areas of life. This increases the unsettling sense of uncertainty that parenting inherently creates. Take consolation from knowing that, with open-minded, compassionate support, your child can thrive. Still, it can be hard to remain patient while waiting for the benefits of your ADHD plan to manifest.

A child's ADHD can affect all family routines. As children become more autonomous, daily family routines get easier. Your time and energy are freed when you no longer need to confirm that your child brushed his teeth or tied his shoes. Unfortunately, ADHD is often like the first falling domino in a line of family logistics. It may feel like no matter how many times you set things aright, the pieces topple again, tipped by ADHD.

Helping a child with ADHD can feel all-consuming. Children with ADHD often require more guidance in completing any daily responsibility. When other kids reach the age where "Please get ready for school" is a viable request, you may still have to guide your child through the steps. Playdates won't offer you a break if you feel you have to stick around in case your child acts out. You may have to devote time to helping your child with homework even when he's in high school. These necessary tasks draw time from everything else you want to do. It also takes extra intention to carve out time for other siblings, your spouse, or your friends.

A child's ADHD can stress a marriage. Parents of children with ADHD experience higher levels of anxiety, depression, and marital strife. They report feeling less capable of changing their child's behavior and describe having fewer positive experiences with their children (Alizadeh and Andries 2002; Kaplan et al. 1998); amidst these difficulties, spouses don't always see eye-to-eye. Sometimes they disagree about the diagnosis of ADHD from the start. Sometimes they don't agree about how to intervene. That leads to even more tension. The damage this causes to marriages is unfortunate; ideally our partnerships should nurture us.

Stress undermines ADHD care, but ADHD increases stress. In essence, ADHD itself gets in the way of your efforts to manage it. It takes time and effort to educate yourself, coordinate with schools and professionals, and develop and maintain a plan, yet your child's ADHD can make it hard for you to find the time and energy. There may never seem to be a good point to pause and start anew. For now, take heart from knowing that the process is like pushing a boulder over a hill. Right now, as you look upslope, it may feel impossible to summon the effort. But eventually you'll experience a time of relative ease, when things start rolling on their own.

Parents of children with ADHD may feel judged by others. If your child had leukemia, would family members or neighbors tell you it doesn't exist? If your child had psoriasis, would others blame you for causing it? If your child had asthma, would you read many articles suggesting that treating the disease ruins children? A child's ADHD uniquely isolates parents. They often end up with an insidious belief that they should be able to do something to make ADHD go away. They wrestle with incredibly difficult choices while also facing other people's opinions about what they should or shouldn't do. Many of these opinions are presented as fact, even when inaccurate or exaggerated. This leaves many parents regretful about their decisions, perhaps even ashamed, along with an entirely inaccurate perception that they caused their child's ADHD, or mismanaged it.

Give Yourself a Break

That sense of judgment about ADHD doesn't just come from other people's comments. Most of us live with a vocal inner critic that provides running commentary about our experience: *I should be able to handle this. I blew it. If only I were better at this, everything would be fine.* If someone else tagged along behind you 24/7 spewing the same stuff in your ear, would you keep that person around? We often cut others slack when they struggle but are enormously harsh and judgmental with ourselves. This negative self-talk heightens reactivity and drags down our mood.

Most thoughts we have are nothing more than thoughts. Some are certainly worth noting. If you think of a task you need to do, take note of it and do it. Maybe you have a thought about a new way to manage a particular situation, or a thought makes you realize you need to have a discussion with someone.

Still, thoughts are often only random ideas with no particular value, a fact that is especially true when it comes to the inner critic. Notice these habitual negative thoughts whenever they come up. Then, without trying to suppress them or chase them away, create distance from the inner critic's insistent commentary by labeling it "only a thought." You might even imagine talking back to this habitual mental chatter: *Thanks for sharing, but that isn't helpful.* Then return to whatever you were doing before the heckling started.

Patiently and repeatedly reminding yourself that your inner critic isn't real will eventually decrease its impact. This frees up your attention to recognize everything else: the successes and happier moments we all encounter.

Taking Care of the Caretaker

Airplane safety announcements often include a statement along the lines of "If oxygen masks are required, secure yours before assisting your child." This makes good sense. If you're short on oxygen, you can't help anyone else. Day-to-day life is the same: if you're not taking good care of yourself, you probably won't be able to help your child as effectively as you otherwise could.

Of course, it's natural to put your child first. Although you'd feel a lot better with a good night's sleep, you get up to calm a child who's had a nightmare. Maybe you'd rather sit outside and read a book, but you drive your child to baseball practice instead. But when you take that approach too far, it becomes counterproductive for everyone. When you're burned out, you aren't at your best.

Burnout due to prolonged stress has been described as a state of exhaustion, cynicism, and inefficacy. It has a negative effect on work, physical health (including risk of heart disease), and mental health. In one study, burned-out people described symptoms identical to those of depression (Hakanen and Schaufeli 2012), and in another study, burnout was associated with cognitive impairments (Beck et al. 2013). We aren't doing ourselves—or our children—any favors if we overlook its effects.

With chronic stress, we feel awful, have less energy, and even experience less compassion. The antithesis of this burned-out feeling is engagement and a sense of positive energy and efficacy. To get anywhere near this more ideal state, we need to remember to put on our own oxygen mask. Here are a few key ways of doing so.

Create and protect time for yourself. Carve out a bit of time daily or weekly to jog, read a book, knit, or do anything you find restorative. Life will try to interfere with even this one healing pursuit, but hold on to it. If you do get wrested away, return to this commitment to yourself as soon and as fully as you're able. If you schedule thirty minutes but only have fifteen, take fifteen. If you want to run three times per week but by Saturday you haven't gone once, don't wait until Monday to start again. Right now, today, find an activity or hobby that keeps you sane and nurtures you.

Create and protect time for your relationships. When people become parents, they often lose time as a couple and time for friends. Reconnecting with your partner for five or ten minutes at the end of the day can be a huge help. Even doing household chores together, like cleaning up after dinner, may be useful. If you have the resources to set up a weekly or monthly date night, commit to it. Also schedule time for friends. Then, when your chosen time or activity arises, try to put other concerns aside for a short while and devote your full attention to the interaction.

Talk about your experience with your child's ADHD. Brain imaging studies show that expressing emotions lessens their power (Lieberman et al. 2007). Therefore, confiding in a friend, relative, or mental health professional will have great benefit beyond problem solving around your child's ADHD.

Actively manage your stress. Stress happens, to paraphrase a common saying. While you may not be responsible for your stress, and you may not be able to eliminate it, skillful stress *management* will help you lessen the impact of the inevitable ups and downs of life. To a certain extent, stress management is about perspective, learning to work with what *is* in life with less resistance; you can surf the waves instead of running right at them and getting slammed into the beach again and again. To manage your stress, use whatever works for you. Anything from exercising regularly and getting good sleep to behavioral therapy to time in nature can also decrease stress. Of course, one of the best studied and most successful stress management methods is mindfulness, which you can develop with the techniques outlined in this book. Whatever you find effective, value it in your daily planning.

Monitor your lifestyle. If you aren't careful about scheduling, life can get busier and busier. Demands rise from many sources: family, friends, household duties, work, and more. After all, you don't want your children to miss out on after-school activities, playdates, and other opportunities. Social media, e-mail, and the like may also steal a lot of your time. The next exercise will help you take steps toward simplifying your life.

Exercise: Decluttering Your Life

It's worthwhile to periodically pause and reassess what your family is devoting time to. What could you cut to simplify life? For this exercise, you'll need three pieces of paper. Blank weekly calendars (download available) would be ideal.

On the first piece of paper, record how you spend your time over a typical week. Really get into the details: Include when everyone wakes and goes to bed and logistics that are unavoidable, like cooking, cleaning, fulfilling your job requirements, and getting your child ready for school. Also estimate how much time you spend checking e-mail, surfing the web, and watching television, as well as time spent on recreation and driving, including driving your child around.

On the second piece of paper, record what you'd like to prioritize for your family. Start with whatever you value most, for both yourself and your child, whether exercise, meditation, connecting with friends or family members, reading, volunteering, creative pursuits, after-school activities, or engaging in fun and positive activities together.

Now, here's the trick: On the third piece of paper, merge the first two into a more ideal schedule. Start with what's nonnegotiable, like household logistics or things you must help your child with. Then fill in what you value most, being sure to include self-care. Then, and only then, use the remaining time for nonessential activities that you don't value as much: yet another after-school activity, video games, or whatever has been consuming your time and your family's.

Take Small, Definitive Steps Toward Change

When setting big goals, it's important to identify smaller, intermediate steps for getting there. For example, if you want to run a marathon but haven't been exercising much, you wouldn't start with an initial goal of running twenty-six miles. You need to start with a short, manageable distance and build from there. Without that kind of methodical plan, you'll give up on big goals before you start.

It's also important to not take on too many different objectives at once. Because your child's ADHD affects many areas of your family life, there are probably many changes you'd like to make. But expecting yourself to tackle too many at once will make the prospect seem impossible.

Focus on setting out a few achievable goals at any given time. This allows for tangible success, which will probably help sustain your motivation and your child's. Here are a few tips for effective goal setting:

- **Practice behavioral triage by setting priorities.** If you don't watch out, a swarm of ideas about what to do to manage your child's ADHD may rattle your brain. You want his school performance to improve, you wish he needed fewer reminders, you'd like him to spend less time playing video games, and more. Write it all down, then actively choose where to start. Focus your planning by taking care of more pressing items first, and then moving down your list over time. (An exercise to help with prioritizing follows shortly.)

- **Emphasize incremental goals.** This is especially important when setting goals for your child. Pick one behavior at a time to target, and break down larger skills, such as getting ready for school, into smaller steps. Maybe the first goal is for your child to get dressed on his own. Then, when that's in place, you can add other aspects of the morning routine, like making a lunch. Take it one step at a time, but keep moving.

- **Monitor success over longer time periods.** Instead of analyzing how each day went, review progress weekly or monthly. Make a note on your calendar so you remember to check your progress, and then forgo day-to-day analysis. Allow for gradual change and the inevitable ups and downs that occur with most changes in life.

- **Keep setting new goals.** You're likely to experience huge relief once you've successfully addressed larger ADHD-related problems, such as academic difficulties or major behavioral issues. This sometimes creates a tendency to settle, giving in on the remaining issues: *It feels so great to no longer be hearing from my child's teachers. I can live with bedtime battles and a messy room.* When life quiets down, enjoy the experience, but keep moving forward with smaller issues. Everything you do to help your child build skills to overcome ADHD will promote his well-being and success throughout life. From time management to sleep routines to cultivating a healthy relationship with technology, continue to seek out and address the more subtle influences of ADHD.

Exercise: Making a Behavioral Triage List

In this exercise, you'll list all of the problems you'd like to address as a first step toward setting priorities. Because this puts so much focus on the negative, let's begin with some reminders of the positive.

List three to five things going well in your life or your own strengths.

1. _____

_____

2. _____

_____

3. _____

_____

4. _____

_____

5. _____

_____

List three to five of your child's strengths. (If you like, revisit the exercise "Accentuating the Positive," in chapter 1.)

1. _____

_____

2. _____

_____

3. _____

_____

4. _____

_____

5. _____

_____

In the space below, list everything you'd like to see improve for your child and your family. Use an additional page if needed.

_____

_____

_____

_____

_____

_____

_____

_____

Now choose one or two of the most disruptive items to work on first. (Upcoming chapters will provide a lot of tools and guidance for doing so.) As best as possible, set aside everything else on the list above for later. Some of it may improve as you and your child learn new skills and techniques for dealing with the first issues. Other things may improve simply because ignoring problematic behaviors is a powerful tool, as discussed in chapter 7.

1. _____

2. _____

Monitor the longer list as life progresses. As you solve the first issues, move new items to the active list and start working on them. In addition, check your own perspective from time to time. Might adjusting your short-term expectations ease some difficulties? Remember, ADHD entails delays in certain skills. Perhaps some of the "problems" you've listed aren't actually inappropriate based on your child's present abilities. Also be sure to revisit your child's strengths from time to time, adding new items as he develops new skills.

Q&A

Q: There's so much information out there about ADHD. How do I know who to believe?

A: Information overload can be part of the stress of parenting a child with ADHD. But there is a large body of science about ADHD, its causes, and treatments. Solidify your own understanding and move past any doubts about ADHD by seeking out reputable sources based in ADHD research. Avoid single voices proclaiming headline-grabbing but fringe ideas. Many people present biased information about ADHD as fact on the Internet and elsewhere, and even major periodicals publish skewed articles that selectively quote research in ways that frighten many readers.

Considering Whether You Have ADHD

Unsurprisingly considering the genetics, many parents of children with ADHD wonder whether they had ADHD or still do, reflected in thoughts like *I probably have a little bit of ADHD myself. I was just like my child when I was a kid.* Witnessing their children benefiting from interventions may spark curiosity about whether they too could benefit. But from there, they often don't give much further thought to what they could do to mitigate the effects of their own ADHD.

This common reaction illustrates the important distinction between acceptance and resignation. "Accepting" means not wrestling with a fact: *I have ADHD, so focusing and organization aren't my strengths. I'll have to take steps to adapt.* "Resignation," on the other hand, often means giving up altogether: *This is who I am. I can't change.*

Could You Have ADHD?

There's an old saw that goes, "The apple doesn't fall far from the tree." Parental ADHD makes managing children's ADHD harder. Therefore, a vital part of caring for your child may be minimizing the impact of your own ADHD. If you believe you may have adult ADHD...

- Complete the Adult ADHD Screening test. (In the Resources section, you'll find information on where you can find the test online.)

- Seek evaluation by a psychologist or psychiatrist familiar with adult ADHD.

- If possible, locate old school records to share with the evaluator.

- Identify someone, such as a partner, friend, or parent, who can act as a corroborating source regarding potential symptoms both now and in the past.

- Recognize that adult ADHD isn't an attention problem alone and explore the impact of executive function, as described in chapter 2, on your own life.

- Collaborate with a doctor or psychologist familiar with ADHD, or an ADHD coach.

- Read books specific to this topic. (See the Resources section at the back of the book.)

The Value of Diagnosis

Simply considering whether you have ADHD can evoke some challenging emotions. You may feel self-recrimination or shame, either for not overcoming ADHD on your own or for not having done anything about it sooner. You may regret that no one knew about your ADHD or helped you with it during your childhood.

However you feel, realize that if you have ADHD, it doesn't define you; it's just one part of you. Nearly everybody has some type of medical condition, from eczema to diabetes. ADHD is no different.

If you're uncertain whether you have ADHD, seek an evaluation. If you do, you can begin to manage it. You can start with many of the techniques in this book, which are equally effective for adults as children. If your ADHD is left unmanaged, you may find it harder to implement what you learn in this book.

Here's the bottom line: With ADHD, by definition you have "impairment" somewhere in life. If you're distractible or a little impulsive but thriving across the board, you don't have ADHD. That said, ADHD can affect self-esteem, daily stress, and relationships, and it can play a role in obesity, financial problems, and procrastination. So if you have potential symptoms, you may be selling yourself short if you don't consider an evaluation.

A diagnosis can provide the "why" behind a lifetime of struggle. It's also a huge step toward understanding how best to move forward. Progress is possible at any age, and assertive ADHD management will decrease your daily stress while potentially increasing both your happiness and your productivity.

Ramifications of Adult ADHD

Adult ADHD affects at least 4 percent of the population, although the actual diagnosis rate is far lower (Kessler et al. 2006). Many adults with ADHD live unaware of what sits behind their chronic struggles with time management, emotional self-regulation, and a host of related faculties that impact family, work, and well-being. They may lack self-confidence or inappropriately judge themselves to be lazy, incompetent, or unmotivated.

Symptoms of adult ADHD can affect the whole family. ADHD can have profound effects on relationships due to its impacts on social interactions and communication style. It can also make it harder to stick to parenting strategies that depend on consistent routines and setting limits, exacerbating an already tough dynamic.

ADHD is inherently a planning disorder. Implementing a new strategy to address your child's ADHD is challenging if you have ADHD yourself, as it can impair your ability to create a plan and stick to it. Take a moment to consider whether you may have symptoms of ADHD like forgetfulness, reactivity, or difficulties with sustaining household routines, persisting with behavioral plans, or keeping track of time, and if so, how they affect your life. Then, when situations potentially related to your own ADHD arise, pause and take a systematic look at the issue through the lens of executive function.

Attention Matters

Paying attention, all on its own, is hugely beneficial for moving beyond living on auto-pilot. But with mindfulness we don't pay attention purely for the sake of paying attention. We also change how we relate to our chaotic inner world.

The brain generates thoughts all the time. Not every idea, fantasy, or feeling is worth validating with a response. Some are worth acting on; some are random, judgmental, or otherwise not so useful. Fearing something bad will happen doesn't make it true. For example, even when you've created a plan for managing your child's ADHD, and even when it's showing positive results, you may be beset by thoughts like *I'll have to keep helping my child with every little thing forever.* Without awareness of this pattern, you can become defined by these internal experiences.

The mind wanders off over and over again. With mindfulness, we practice guiding it back, a process that influences how often we choose what to focus on. And with ongoing practice, we also can come back sooner each time we're distracted. Then, because anything we practice repetitively rewires the brain, this new perspective becomes part of our underlying neurology. In this way, we can more fully enjoy what there is to enjoy and more easily manage the rest: *Right now, I'm going to give full attention to my child. Later I'll plan tomorrow's meeting.*

If you feel skeptical, consider this: research shows that, among people with ADHD, mindfulness practice is associated with an improved ability to focus and shift attention. They experience improvements in stress levels, attention, and measures of executive function after eight weeks or less of training (Zylowska et al. 2008). The brain responds to repetition the same way as the body responds to physical exercise, and anyone at any age will benefit from working on cognitive fitness in this way.

How Attention Can Help You Get Unstuck from Stress

Some of our mental overload and stress is due to where we place our attention. For example, we may be ruminating about the past or projecting into the future. Something that happened before or may happen later nags at us, and we can't let go. Meanwhile, life is going on right here, at this moment, nowhere else. And the present moment often isn't half bad, even when our attention is stuck somewhere else.

We can also get caught up in thinking that problems are fixed and unchanging: *This is who my child is and will always be. This is a situation I've never had a handle on, and l never will.* Yet nothing in life is unchanging, and with skillful effort we can influence much of what happens.

The simple practice of choosing where to place our attention and then coming back to that focus again and again lays the groundwork for profound change. Any moment we're actually paying attention is an opportunity to choose what we do next. The next exercise will help you start to devote that kind of attention to your experience of stress.

Exercise: Attending to Your Experience of Stress

Turning some attention to your own stress response will allow you to notice and address it earlier, short-circuiting a cycle in which negative thoughts lead to emotions (and vice versa), which lead to body sensations, which lead to more negative thoughts, on and on. When you notice those experiences as they arise, you can break the cycle.

Take some time to reflect on your experience of stress. Then, in the space below, describe how it affects your body, thoughts, emotions, and behaviors. If you aren't sure, try calling a recent stressful experience to mind and imagining it in detail. If you're still unsure, monitor your experience of stress over several days, and then come back to complete this exercise.

Physical sensations: _____

_____

_____

Thought patterns: _____

_____

_____

Emotional states: _____

_____

_____

Habitual behaviors when stressed: _____

_____

_____

Practice: Paying More Attention to the Joys of Life

We often breeze through pleasurable times without giving them a moment's thought. For example, you may be so annoyed that your child forgot to make his bed that you don't even notice that it's a beautiful day outside. Increasing your awareness refocuses your attention on what's going well, separate from the pull of anxiety or anything else that amplifies your stress.

Anytime you choose, you can practice mindfulness by immersing yourself in something you enjoy: *Here I am, reading to my daughter at bedtime. This is what it feels like to snuggle together. This is what her hair smells like. This is her laugh. This is what it reminds me of from my past, and this is where my mind goes into the future. And here I am, back in this room, reading to my daughter at bedtime.*

As you start to devote more attention to positive experiences, you may notice another aspect of how the brain works: there's often a sense of regret tied to enjoyment. You may worry about the good time ending. You may start thinking about how your daughter will grow up and move away. You may fear forgetting this precious moment. This attachment to holding on to things as they are right now causes stress too.

For this practice, pay specific attention to one pleasurable experience each day. When your mind wanders, return your attention to the experience. Notice sounds, physical sensations, emotions, and thoughts. Here's a log you can use to record your experience (download available).

Event	Sounds	Physical sensations	Emotions	Thoughts

Make Time for Self-Care

It's common for people to feel that they don't have even a moment for themselves. Here's a mental game for playing with this perception: If someone offered you $10,000 for each time you took fifteen minutes to meditate, go for a run, or hang out with a friend, could you make it happen? How about $10,000 to leap over your own house? That last one is impossible, but making time for yourself is a surmountable challenge.

Proactively pick a time and place to get started with self-care. Remind yourself that taking time for yourself benefits your family. Don't wait for the hour, week, month, or year when things feel quiet. It may never happen. Also, don't get attached to an ideal, such as that only a long run (not a short one) is worthwhile, or only a full vacation (not a half hour in the park) will have value. Taking even just a few minutes for a cup of tea or a quiet moment will be beneficial on a busy day.

Parenting can be a humbling and overwhelming experience. We plan and predict and laugh with and love our children, but there are countless unexpected events we can't avoid. However, we can aim to teach our children the basic skills for handling life's ups and downs with equanimity and wisdom. To that end, we need to cultivate these traits in ourselves first.

Action Plan: Caring for the Caregiver

Getting started on a new approach to managing your child's ADHD may feel overwhelming. Your busy, stressful life continues while you attempt to develop and maintain an effective strategy. You can't put aside all of life and focus solely on your child's ADHD. But you can, at any moment in time, try something new and start your family down a different path. Attending to your own self-care is an essential part of the journey.

- ☐ Identify something that helps keep you sane. Write it here, and be vigilant about making time for it:

_____

- ☐ Create time for important personal relationships.

- ☐ Simplify life whenever possible and avoid overscheduling.

- ☐ Keep working on managing your child's ADHD. Deal with the big issues first, then explore and address all of the nuanced ways ADHD affects everyday life.

- ☐ Set short-term, realistic goals for change.

- ☐ Take a moment to settle yourself several times each day, using the STOP practice to help you make a deliberate choice about what to do next.

- ☐ Pay attention to enjoyable experiences when they happen.

- ☐ Schedule a daily guided mindfulness practice.

Chapter 4

Change Starts with You

Read this chapter to...

- Understand that parents are the driving force for creating change in children with ADHD

- Implement support systems that encourage your child to develop life skills while also making your household run more smoothly

- Use mindfulness to support ADHD care by decreasing your reactivity and increasing your flexibility in solving problems

Demanding as it is, parents essentially serve as a child's executive function while her skills are developing. You have to plan and organize for your child until she catches up. Children don't yet have the perspective to develop a nuanced plan, reflect on their growth, and adjust the plan as needed.

Consider this example: Your child sits, engrossed, playing a video game. You yell from across the house, "Ten minutes until the bus comes!" But because of her ADHD, she can't smoothly transition her attention from the game to hearing your voice. She mumbles a reply but doesn't register what you said. Nine minute later you find that she's still playing. Your bile rises as you turn off the computer. Flustered, she screams, "I hate you," and starts to cry.

In contrast, if you keep executive function in mind, it could go like this: Your child sits, engrossed, playing a video game. Aware that her school bus will arrive soon, you engage her: "Please pause the game and save it now. The bus is coming soon." She keeps playing, so you step closer to gain her attention. Your frustration mounts, but you have a recourse: you've worked with her to set up a reward chart (explained in chapter 6), and one thing she can earn a point for is "listening on the first try." So you say, "I'm going to count to three, and after that you won't earn your point for listening this morning. Let's make sure you do." Intense grumbling follows, but she stops playing. You add, "Great job on listening. Now let's get you to school on time!"

The only choice you directly control in any moment is yours. However, your words and actions can potentially escalate or de-escalate any situation, reinforcing certain patterns and diminishing others. You didn't cause your child's ADHD, but you can profoundly influence what happens next in each moment. And whatever has occurred in the past, you can define a new way forward.

Developing a New Relationship to Difficult Experiences

Through mindfulness practice, you may be starting to see that a thought is just a thought—it isn't innately good or bad, it's just a passing mental event to consider. In the same way, an ADHD symptom is just an ADHD symptom, no more and no less. If your child currently cannot remember her morning routine when pressured, manage her frustration, or deal with other experiences related to her ADHD, then she cannot. This may exasperate you both, but it remains true in that moment. Long-term change is possible, but in any moment, ADHD can have an impact you may not be able to alter quite yet.

Your feelings about your child's ADHD are also whatever they are today, even though you may feel frustrated with your own frustration. Acceptance doesn't mean forcing yourself to say "It's all good" about anything; you feel whatever you feel. Further, thinking you should be more accepting and at peace than you actually are is likely to make your experience even harder.

Unpleasant events are part of life for most people, including parents of children with ADHD. Your child struggles with self-management and emotion regulation, and that affects you. By building your capacity to give your child your complete attention, even in unpleasant moments, you can see the nuances of her ADHD more clearly and will be more likely to make skillful choices. As you begin to grasp the full influence of ADHD and approach your child differently, you can send the day in a new direction.

How We Compound Unpleasant Experiences

Even the most unpleasant experience is rarely as straightforward as it looks at first. Consider jet lag. There's nothing nice about it. You fly overseas for a business conference, and the next day you feel physically and emotionally drained.

But is that all? You may also become fearful that a meeting you have later in the day will go poorly because you're tired. You may chastise yourself for not flying earlier to adapt. You may be nagged by stressful thoughts about returning home: *I'm going to be here long enough to adjust to this time zone. Then when I go home, I'll feel awful for work on Monday.*

Maybe you arrive at your meeting and a key contact seems tense and distant. So you start worrying about that: *She's not going for our proposal. She's hardly listening.* The mental chorus crescendos until you become completely frazzled. Yet in reality, the meeting has barely started, and if she is tense and distant, it could be for many reasons. Perhaps her father has the flu. The fact that you're wiped out distorts your perceptions.

You're jet-lagged. That's enough. Next time you might choose to fly in earlier or give yourself more time on your return home. Right now you're guiding the meeting, and you know you've prepared well. Recognizing all that, ask yourself: what would serve the situation best?

Exercise: Exploring the Details of Unpleasant Experiences

With anything we encounter, the details are often more subtle than our impressions. Now consider the typical ADHD challenges you face with your child. What is the actual reality of your experience? What's the reality of your child's experience? Where do fearful thoughts about the future or regrets about the past add intensity to the experience? How does your emotional state affect the situation?

In this exercise, you'll explore these questions in regard to a specific unpleasant experience. Select any recent or recurring unpleasant situation you face, not necessarily choosing the most challenging one that comes to mind at first. Explore it below, describing specific aspects of your experience while cultivating a more nuanced perspective on it.

Unpleasant experience: _____

_____

_____

Thoughts while it happened: _____

_____

_____

Emotions while it happened: _____

_____

Body sensations while it happened: _____

_____

Thoughts, emotions, and body sensations now, just thinking about it: _____

_____

_____

_____

_____

The experience of stress is usually more complicated than it seems on the surface. Countless thoughts, emotions, and physical sensations, many below the conscious level, fuel the fire. Something unpleasant happens, and we internally compound its effects. Without trying to change anything, explore what happens when you simply bring more awareness to the varied aspects of your experience.

Seizing the Reins

When a child lags behind her peers in speaking, adults instinctually adjust their own language and expectations. If a child is slow in learning to walk, they offer support without prodding her to catch up all at once. For children with ADHD, delayed performance or age-inappropriate behavior is often misattributed to lack of effort or not caring. Yet as with any developmental delay, ADHD requires that adults create appropriate interventions that can help children find their way.

It's normal that parents living with ADHD may feel frustrated, disappointed, or overwhelmed by a child's behavior, but a general concept holds true: if you expect something new to happen *today* without changing your approach, you're likely to increase your suffering. If your child's ADHD causes some kind of challenge that comes up repeatedly, you need to address it to create an opportunity for change.

By releasing expectations about what's age appropriate, you can recognize your child's capabilities as they currently are. While kids may outgrow certain issues with enough time, you can't expect more rapid progress without an effective plan. Instead of wrestling with how your child should be or should act, you can frame ADHD as a delay in acquiring a particular skill set.

One common trigger of problematic behavior is asking a child with ADHD to do something beyond her current capabilities. If she can't get ready for school without reminders, expecting her to do so will lead to a battle. If scholastic demands overestimate her present level of independence in completing assignments, she'll struggle in school. On the other hand, if you do nothing more than adjust the environment to help your child manage her ADHD, behavioral and academic improvements will follow.

Seeing ADHD as a disorder of self-management that manifests uniquely for each child allows for clear-sighted parenting. Whether your child has trouble shifting attention when playing, has a horrendously messy room, or never manages to bring the right books home to complete homework assignments, remember that these behaviors are symptoms of ADHD. Rather than punishing such behavior, you can develop a plan to support your child's success in overcoming it.

From what we say and how we say it to what we do and choose not to do, all our actions have implications. This fact underlies basic behavior management strategies. You can reinforce and strengthen appropriate behaviors with positive feedback (covered in chapter 6). You can decrease undesired behaviors by ignoring them or offering corrective feedback (covered in chapter 7). These actions will educate your child by creating consistent messages about the effects of her choices. In this way, you can seize the reins from ADHD.

Practice: Fifteen Breaths

As you journey deeper into understanding your child's ADHD and learning to manage it, continue to remain aware of yourself. Notice when you feel agitated, shut down, or exhausted. Those feelings may come and go, but they're as real as the neurology of ADHD. In the midst of building a plan to manage your child's ADHD, continue to emphasize the work you began in the previous chapter: taking care of yourself.

Finding even a few moments of downtime to rest, exercise, or talk with a friend can be challenging for a parent. Another way to carve out a break is to take fifteen mindful breaths (Gunaratana 2014); it only takes about sixty seconds. When you begin feeling rattled or exhausted, or when transitioning from one part of your day to the next, there's almost always a minute to be had.

To do this practice, focus on your next fifteen breaths without striving to make anything happen beyond observing and letting go. Expect distracted thoughts and everything else that tugs at you. When your mind drifts, come back to wherever you left off counting. In an unforced way, bring your attention back to the moment and your breathing as often as need be.

So much of anxiety and mental fatigue stems from getting hooked by thoughts: to-do lists, fears, regrets, and on and on. The mind has a hard time letting go of whatever feels off. Without trying to suppress these thoughts, practice letting go of them for a moment. Amidst a hectic day, allow yourself the opportunity to not do or plan or fix anything for fifteen breaths. In this mindful minute, you can regroup and redirect yourself.

Fostering Independence

To help your child move past the hurdles of ADHD, you need to create short-term safety nets and long-term plans for independence. Initially, you may assume all executive function roles, even for a high school student. If your child is falling behind and failing tenth grade, you may need to redesign her academic plan. And during the time it takes for this new plan to come together and be effective, you must meticulously guide her in staying caught up day to day.

For example, forgetfulness is a symptom of ADHD. If your child can't remember to hand in her homework, it's your job (perhaps in collaboration with a teacher or ADHD professional) to figure out a solution. By creating reminders, you avoid the ineffective recourse of arguing again and again. And as those reminders take effect and create new habitual behavior, you can hand responsibility back to your child.

While parents sometimes fear these supports will act as a crutch, they actually allow children to assume more responsibility with time. You encourage hard work and appropriate behavior. You create systems that teach new skills. And by recognizing the broad influence of ADHD in this way, you help your child develop confidence and flourish.

A detailed program created and maintained by adults doesn't make a child with ADHD dependent; it allows for success. Children with ADHD can become overwhelmed in the absence of adult support. They lack the planning skills to overcome ADHD on their own. Guiding your child toward small successes will lead to larger victories, and both independence and motivation will follow.

Typical teen development increases the challenge. Teenagers resist adult involvement as they aim to become more independent. Paradoxically, they also want to be part of the pack, syncing with their peers on everything from fashion choices to interests to attitudes. Because of their desire to fit in with their peers, they may deny having medical conditions that potentially set them apart, whether ADHD, diabetes, or anything in between.

But here's the catch: teens with ADHD usually don't have the mature self-awareness or logistical skills to manage their ADHD on their own. With younger children, you can generally put strategies in place without your child directly contributing. With teens, you need to aim for collaboration, even when they sometimes resist. Here are a few tips that may help:

- Encourage communication and discussion when possible, listening to your teen's recommendations and integrating them when feasible.

- Offer options between valid choices: "You can have an extra help session at lunch or have one after school."

- Compromise whenever reasonable, but not in ways that impair your teen's chances of overcoming ADHD.

- Use rewards (discussed in chapter 6) to encourage compliance with the plan.

- Help your teen identify a tutor, psychologist, or ADHD coach to collaborate with if she resists parental involvement.

Executive Function Management Tool Kit

Adults affect the course of a child's ADHD both through their own actions and by adapting the environment to help her manage her own ADHD. This concept, called externalizing the system, was first described by ADHD expert Russell Barkley (2006). It means using routines, lists, alarms, and anything else necessary to avoid relying on executive function skills that aren't yet in place. This approach helps households run with less effort and can also minimize the impact of poor executive function on anyone progressing into adult ADHD.

Having realistic expectations that acknowledge your child's ADHD will ease everyday logistics and make your child more likely to succeed in any task. As you more effectively meet your child's needs in her struggle with executive function, many family tensions will defuse. And when you adjust your own behavior accordingly, life will become easier for you and everyone else.

The following guidelines will help you get started on managing your child's ADHD through the lens of executive function. As a reminder, the six executive function skill groups are attention management, action management, task management, information management, emotion management, and effort management. Note that there's no need to follow all the recommendations below. Not everyone with ADHD struggles with all executive function difficulties or has the same patterns of difficulties. Select those that seem most appropriate for your child and your family, and be sure to create visible reminders of the plan to keep everyone on track.

Helping Your Child with Attention Management

The topic of attention and ADHD is complicated. As discussed, children with ADHD aren't just distractible. Sometimes they have a hard time sustaining focus when cognitive demands rise. Other times, they may hyperfocus and have difficulty transitioning their attention. Here are some techniques to help your child with attention management:

- Obtain your child's full attention before making requests. Wait for a pause in what she's doing or use a verbal or physical cue, such as a gentle hand on the shoulder.

- Transition attention whenever possible. Give a heads-up and use countdowns ("Ten minutes until bedtime," then "Five minutes until bedtime," and so on). Be sure you have her attention before giving the warning.

- Use timers to help focus attention. For example, break up schoolwork into manageable segments or give an end point to tasks like cleaning up. The latter can even be a kind of game: "Let's see if we can get everything put away in two minutes!"

- Minimize distractions by setting up a clutter-free work space away from toys and television.

- Establish homework environments and work spaces that allow for adult supervision. Hopefully a central location can be devoted to the task at hand—probably not your child's bedroom, but also not a table in a busy kitchen.

- Get your child involved in activities that build sustained focus and attention, such as yoga, mindfulness practice, or games like chess. (Chapter 11 is devoted to working with children on mindfulness.)

- Manage screen time. Although technology can be entertaining and is perhaps helpful for organization, it's a common distraction and a significant concern for many children with ADHD. (This topic is covered in detail in chapter 10.)

Helping Your Child with Action Management

One of the more complicated aspects of ADHD to live with is hyperactivity, fidgeting, impulsiveness, and difficulties with self-monitoring of behavior in general. It's helpful to remember that these are simply ADHD symptoms and not yet fully under your child's control. Even so, it can be exhausting and disruptive until you implement a successful plan. While these symptoms persist, here are a few tips for managing them:

- Create behavioral plans that use praise, rewards, and limits to build skills in self-monitoring of behavior (covered in chapters 6 and 7).

- Encourage your child to use the STOP practice throughout the day. This practice creates a moment of reflection that can help your child manage her activities.

- Plan breaks. Balance the short-term reality of ADHD with long-term goals. Repeated arguments over a child's fidgeting won't accomplish anything and will frustrate everyone involved. Create a planned break so your child can burn off this energy. For example, when dining out, a brief running session outside the restaurant between courses may ease the problem.

- Schedule regular exercise breaks throughout your child's day. Make sure she gets to participate in school recess and that it includes physical activity. Prioritize active after-school activities. Get your child out on the playground, play active games in the yard, or run fun races together.

Q&A

Q: If ADHD involves delays in development of executive function, why treat it at all? Don't children catch up eventually?

A: Executive function skills evolve over many years, and some children outgrow ADHD. Most experience an overall diminishment of at least some symptoms, particularly around activity level and impulsivity. But these changes occur slowly, over many years. Executive function is required for social development and classroom learning. It also allows for healthy self-esteem, confidence, and emotional resilience. If you let five or ten years pass while hoping your child will outgrow ADHD, this could derail other aspects of her development. Early intervention will minimize the impact of ADHD both in the formative years and throughout life.

Helping Your Child with Task Management

Task management becomes the core impairment for many people with ADHD, especially as they approach adulthood. The need for independence rises with every passing year, but developmental skills lag behind. A high school senior with the planning ability of a twelve-year-old will benefit from adult support even if she resists or school policy dictates otherwise. Having a realistic sense of a child's task management skills is intrinsic to effective long-term ADHD management. More concretely, here are a few techniques you can use to support your child in task management:

- Set alarms and have adults provide reminders. For children with ADHD, keeping track of time and what they need to get done is an ongoing challenge, so external cues are very helpful.

- Break larger tasks into smaller parts, with due dates and timelines. The understanding that lengthy assignments require many small actions steps seems instinctual if you have strong executive function, but it doesn't come naturally for those with ADHD.

- Schedule everything that must happen. Because children with ADHD have impaired time awareness, open-ended scheduling ("You need to study sometime this weekend") is a setup for failure. Children with ADHD routinely forget, avoid, or otherwise fail to attend to anything that isn't firmly scheduled. Put everything from study time to chores on your child's calendar.

- Maintain consistent routines. (This is addressed in detail in chapter 10.) Although this can be difficult to sustain, especially if a parent has ADHD, it is perhaps the most vital approach to making a home run smoothly and teaching children life skills. Use written or illustrated step-by-step lists for any routine at any age. Even when kids know the details by heart, ADHD symptoms cause them to lose track. Rather than expecting them to remember everything, emphasize using lists; this will create a helpful lifelong habit.

- Transition your child toward independence. Routines teach organization, so make a habit of asking your child, "Have you used the list?" Instead of prompting her to do each item separately, reinforce self-monitoring by directing your child to her list until she consistently refers to it on her own. Post lists where she'll see them: in her bedroom, in the kitchen and bathroom, and so on. For a child in middle school or older, gradually increase her involvement in planning her daily and weekly calendar, discussing details of time management and scheduling.

Organization, Executive Function, and Planning

The impact of ADHD on planning and problem solving can be subtle. Consider this example: A teacher assigns a book report. He provides a list of titles to select from, divides the project into individual due dates (read the book by one date, outline it by another, and write the report by a third), and monitors student progress along the way.

This plan seems perfect, yet for a child with ADHD, executive function deficits can crop up in perhaps unexpected ways. For example, even "Choose a book" can trip up a child. As she looks into potential choices, she may research each book in-depth online without coming to a decision, or fritter away the evening reading the first option she comes across.

To implement a strong planning approach for your child, you need to create an initial strategy and then adapt it based on her response. So, returning to that example, the next time around that student would receive coaching from a parent or teacher on picking a book.

For any ADHD-related plan, take definable steps, then remain open to adapting as needed based on the results. When you see what you thought was a well-made plan coming apart at the seams, pause and take a few breaths—or more. Then reassess the plan through the lens of your child's executive function abilities.

Helping Your Child with Information Management

The mental ability to sort through, organize, and manage information depends on executive function, as does the ability to take what we've learned and efficiently use it in problem solving, conversation, or writing. Even holding on to short-term requests relies on strong information management, so for children with ADHD, follow-through on both requests and classroom learning may be challenging. Here are a few tips to help your child with information management:

- Keep requests simple and short, and make them one step at a time if necessary. One common source of perceived oppositional behavior is when a child sent off for a bunch of tasks ends up somewhere else entirely. Request one or two steps, monitor for completion, and then move on to the next steps.

- Put requests in writing. As with maintaining a routine, provide your child with written or picture lists for requests that require multiple steps.

- Any unfamiliar task relies on information management for problem solving and figuring things out. Prioritize your child's acquisition of basic, foundational skills in reading, writing, and math. Fluency in these areas will reduce the demands on her executive function skills in learning environments.

Helping Your Child with Emotion Management

Kids with ADHD don't melt down or blow up out of choice. Tantrums, poor frustration tolerance, whining, and other symptoms of emotional immaturity reflect a delay in acquiring emotion-management skills. Of course, these behaviors are stressful for everyone. They're challenging and disruptive. Also be aware that they aren't anyone's fault, even when they occur in public and it feels like everyone's staring and your inner critic leaps into action. And although they aren't your fault, you can support your child in learning to manage her emotions. Here are a few techniques for doing so:

- Use behavioral techniques that discourage inappropriate behavior (more on this in chapters 6 and 7). While empathetically recognizing that your child feels upset, set boundaries around how she acts.

- Practice behavioral triage, setting priorities and working on the most significant behaviors (hitting) before moving on to less acute problems (rolling on the floor unresponsively).

- Anticipate difficult situations and discuss them with your child. Provide options for appropriate behavior in advance, using words and behaviors that de-escalate the situation: "Next time you feel yourself getting angry, you can take a break and go to your room until you're calm again."

- Practice emotion labeling. Help your child learn to identify and describe emotions through discussion and how you describe your own experience, and using kids' books on this topic. Verbally labeling emotions diminishes their impact.

- Have your child work with a psychologist. One-on-one training can be just as helpful for emotion management as for skills like hitting a curve ball or learning to play the trumpet.

- Encourage your child to use the STOP practice when she begins to get upset, angry, or otherwise rattled. Many years ago in the *New York Times*, an elementary school student described mindfulness as meaning "not hitting someone in the mouth" when upset (P. L. Brown 2007). The STOP practice is one way to encourage that perspective.

Helping Your Child with Effort Management

ADHD undermines the ability to sustain engagement, particularly with activities that require ongoing cognitive effort or long-term planning. The complex difficulties children with ADHD face in motivation and effort call for nuanced support from parents and teachers alike. Here are a few strategies that can be useful:

- Encourage sustained effort through praise and rewards. Increase motivation through positive feedback, even if you feel your child should be able to complete a task on her own. Use a reward chart (described in chapter 6) to establish a collaborative approach rather than arguing: "You'll earn a point when you've finished your homework." In this way, you assist your child in moving toward a success.

- Modify homework so it consumes a reasonable amount of time. Though not followed nowadays in many schools, ten minutes per grade is the national recommendation: no more than twenty minutes in second grade, sixty in sixth grade, and so on. As you'll learn in chapter 8, the main point of homework is to reinforce classroom learning and teach some responsibility, nothing more.

- Alternate timed periods of work with timed breaks to help your child sustain attention.

- Allow extra time (or don't time tasks at all). If time pressure undermines your child's performance, remove the barrier by allowing more time in the first place.

Letting Go of Perfectionism

The idea that, as a parent, you influence your child's ADHD is a loaded one. Just because both you and your child need to develop certain skills and change habits doesn't mean you're at fault. And even if you're capable of describing optimum parenting of a child with ADHD in great detail, this doesn't mean you can sustain that ideal.

The concept of "perfect" itself often triggers a negative mental cycle. If you're aware that you ideally would have said or done something different than you did, the added weight of judging yourself for not handling the situation perfectly will amplify your suffering. Consciously or subconsciously, you also may judge your child for not fitting your definition of "perfect," or you may worry that your parents, friends, or neighbors are judging you for your child's "imperfect" behavior. Perfection is unattainable, so if you strive for it, you doom yourself to falling short.

Sometimes these judgments extend to life itself. Maybe you have an expectation about family gatherings and think every Thanksgiving should mirror your image of family happiness, with smiling faces gathered around the table and everyone getting along swimmingly. Then reality becomes a crisis as people bicker, kids sneak off, and the turkey is dry.

When you let go of expecting things, yourself included, to be perfect, space opens up to enjoy whatever has gone well. You can also recover more quickly when, inevitably, things don't go as you imagined. Returning to the Thanksgiving example, perhaps everyone came together and mostly had a good time, so the only way the holiday wasn't a success was in comparison to how you felt things should have been.

No one handles everything like a parent from a 1950s sitcom—cheerful, unflappable, and wise. Still, as you devote yourself to living with more awareness and parenting more mindfully, it can be all too easy to slip into self-blame when you don't live up to your ideals: *If I were a better parent, I would implement everything I'm reading about to manage my child's ADHD all at once. I wouldn't shout. I would have gotten my child diagnosed three years ago...* This judgmental mental habit creates more stress. We're all flawed, struggling, and doing our best. Letting go of perfectionism can go a long way toward making your path as a parent easier.

By practicing awareness of the convoluted, confusing life we all experience, you familiarize yourself with reactive habits and assumptions, like self-judgment, that resurface again and again. If you educate yourself, without harshness, about your parenting habits, they will steer your life less often. You may realize more quickly when you've checked out and come back to yourself and your child that much sooner. Each time you recognize the inner shouting that you've been less than perfect, pause, watch it pass like a summer storm, and return to the joy and chaos of life exactly as it is. The practice that follows will help you with this.

Practice: Watching the Weather

Much of our experience comes and goes regardless of what we think or do. But instead of recognizing that reality, we tire ourselves out and increase stress by wrestling with it, typically with about as much effectiveness as trying to chase away a monsoon. To build discernment—the ability to differentiate between what you can and cannot change in your life—it's useful to practice observing all of your experiences like watching clouds pass in the sky.

Initially, you might do this practice for ten minutes. Set a timer so you won't be watching the clock.

Sit comfortably in a chair or lie on your back. Allow your eyes to close or place your vision somewhere unexciting. Observing your breath, recognize that it will continue all day long without you needing to do anything about it. Your breath is an ever-present anchor for your attention, so when your mind wanders during this practice, use breathing to guide yourself back.

During this practice, and throughout the day, various inner experiences show up, such as thoughts and emotions. Right now, simply notice and observe what arises as though it were a neutral phenomenon outside yourself, like the weather.

Noticing thoughts, allow them to arise and pass without engaging them. At some other time, you might problem solve, set something aright, or pursue something new and creative. For now, just watch thoughts arise and then pass. Anything important enough to require attention will be there when you're done.

Emotions may arise in the same way—relaxation, boredom, restlessness, excitement, or others. They may relate to something you're experiencing. Quite often they appear on their own, for no clear reason, and then pass.

As if you were looking out a window watching a storm develop and then fade away, practice observing thoughts, emotions, and whatever else you encounter. For just these few minutes, let things be.

The intention of mindfulness is not escape. In fact, by observing your experience in this way, sometimes you may stumble onto aspects of your experience you'd otherwise ignore. Emotions or thoughts you might have avoided or simply missed may suddenly seem clear. And there is always value in creating space between what you observe and what you choose to do about it—something you can cultivate through this practice of watching the weather of your experience.

Rippling the Surface of ADHD

Picture this: As you're with your child waiting for the bus in the morning, you smile. You joke around and she laughs. How might that influence not just her feelings, but her behavior toward a child sitting across the aisle on the way to school?

Conversely, imagine that your morning routine has gone poorly. Frustrated and amped up, you frown and distractedly kiss your child on the head. Then you sternly say, "Don't forget to hand in your homework *again*," and turn away.

How might she now behave? While your actions aren't immediately responsible for whatever happens on the bus, they do have influence. They affect not only your child, but the people she encounters throughout her day.

Overwhelming as it can feel, this cause-and-effect relationship is good news. Small changes are always possible, and they can lead to big benefits over weeks, months, or years. When we're on autopilot, things happen to us and because of us without our awareness. By devoting increased attention and intention to your actions, you can become an agent of the positive changes you'd like to see.

Exercise: Reframing Behavioral and Academic Challenges

For any aspect of life, consider how delayed executive function might impair your child's experience and what kind of support you can provide. For example, if she can't shift attention well enough to register what you're saying when she's playing a video game, how could you get her attention first?

Rather than having an expectation of perfect behavior, use the tools in this chapter to find new ways to manage entrenched situations. There's no need to fit concerns about your child exactly into one executive function box or another. Many challenges can be eased by providing support for multiple cognitive skills, so consider each of the six areas as you engage in creative problem solving.

For this exercise, choose one of the current action items on your behavioral triage list. Then consult the lists of helpful strategies in the Executive Function Management Tool Kit earlier in this chapter to identify techniques you can use to address that issue. More specific action plans for various topics follow in later chapters. For now, view ADHD as a developmental delay of executive function and consider how you might adjust your own actions and expectations first.

Behavioral or academic concern: _____

_____

_____

Ways I can support attention management: _____

_____

_____

_____

Ways I can support action management: _____

_____

_____

_____

Ways I can support task management: _____

_____

_____

_____

Ways I can support information management: _____

_____

_____

_____

Ways I can support emotion management: _____

_____

_____

_____

Ways I can support effort management: _____

_____

_____

_____

Action Plan: Externalizing the System

Now that you have a number of tools for supporting your child in overcoming executive function challenges, you can start taking concrete steps toward change. Remember, although your child needs to put in solid effort, you can't expect her skills to be other than what they are right now. For change to happen, you need to adjust the environment, teach her new skills, or intervene in some other way.

☐ Select an initial target from your behavioral triage list. It's fine to use the same one you selected for the last exercise in this chapter. Write it here:

_____

☐ Choose techniques from the Executive Function Management Tool Kit in this chapter to begin applying. Write them here:

_____

_____

☐ Continue to dedicate yourself to daily mindfulness practice. Your resilience, responsiveness, and attentiveness will grow in tandem with the effort you put into your practice over time.

☐ Use the Fifteen Breaths and STOP practices throughout your day to step out of operating on autopilot.

☐ Create reminders about both the new ADHD techniques you intend to use and your mindfulness practice:

   ☐ Post reminders in places where you'll see them often.

   ☐ Set alarms on your computer or smartphone reminding you of your plan. Anticipate stressful times, such as homework, bedtime, or morning routines, and program reminders to pop up at those times.

   ☐ Seek support from others in reminding you of your intentions. Discuss them with your partner, a close friend, your therapist, or someone else you trust.

☐ Return to your plans for managing your child's ADHD and practicing mindfulness as often as needed, and without giving yourself a hard time. New habits take a long time to become ingrained. When you forget to follow through or you try something that doesn't work right away, return and readjust.

Chapter 5

Listen Closely and Hear the Effects of ADHD on Communication

Read this chapter to...

- Recognize the effects of ADHD on communication and understand how to manage them

- Monitor the influence of your own behavior on communication with your child

- Use mindfulness to support clear, strong communication skills

Our minds produce a constant patter—or deluge—of thoughts, not all of which are entirely useful. Many ideas and assumptions we have about ourselves, others, and the world around us feel like facts. Maybe we believe the judgmental inner voice that says, *I blew it again* or *Everyone is watching me.* Maybe we suspect a hidden agenda when our teen says, "Can I stay at Joey's house on Saturday night?" We often give even the most random thoughts and emotions free rein to influence our lives.

When you attend to your mental chatter, you'll begin to notice when you've been triggered before a series of reactions tumble forth. You might then pause for a moment and avoid well-worn neurological ruts, realizing, *I'm feeling rattled right now. I'd better take care with what I say next.* You can also begin to see the difference between your inner critic beating you up (*I'm awful; what was I thinking?*) and acknowledging that you've erred (*I said that poorly*).

When you don't attend to your experience in this way, something can fluster you and initiate a stress response without you ever noticing what started it. You can end up trapped in impotent silence or reacting to scattershot emotions and entirely unable to engage in creative problem solving, all because of something outside your awareness that sent you into stress mode.

When you're on autopilot, habitual patterns will inevitably influence how you act and speak. An unconscious expectation that all seven-year-old boys can sit through a meal will lead to frustration each and every time yours gets up from his seat. But if you notice that trigger, you can set off down a different path, maybe allowing him a break from the table, rewarding him if he does stay seated, or letting the behavior slide for a while. Suddenly, everyone gets along better at dinnertime. That type of change starts from being aware in the first place.

Finding the Middle Ground

No matter how out of control, uninterested, or irrational your child acts at a given point in time, what you do or say can potentially escalate or de-escalate the situation. These choices also teach your child lessons in conflict management and influence how he communicates. You can always dominate by yelling louder, or by resorting to sarcasm or silence, but that will teach your child that the loudest voice, or the most biting or least responsive, wins. Yet not standing your ground reinforces another set of maladaptive patterns. A middle ground exists where you can both stand up for your beliefs and conduct yourself in a way that facilitates effective, calm communication.

How ADHD Affects Communication

Executive function allows us to sort through the barrage of information we encounter every day, from paying attention to the right voice in a classroom to organizing responses during a rapidly paced discussion. Children who are delayed in these skills miss what's being asked of them and have a hard time expressing themselves. From the living room to the classroom, you can make both your life and your child's life easier by actively considering how ADHD affects communication. To enhance your ability to communicate in ways that will work well for your child, let's take a look at exactly how ADHD affects communication.

Speech Fluency

Research shows that children with ADHD are at risk for articulation disorders, which affect the ability to produce specific sounds when speaking (Kim and Kaiser 2000). Studies have even found that these speech difficulties may be correlated with risk for ADHD (Cohen et al. 1998; Lewis et al. 2012). Beyond that, children with ADHD commonly have differences in fluency and vocal quality when speaking. Compared to peers with learning disabilities alone, children with ADHD showed increased volume and variability in pitch when talking, along with patterns such as an increased number of vocal pauses (Breznitz 2003).

Children with ADHD tend to produce more vocal repetition or word fillers as they try to organize their thoughts, somewhat similar to a stammer. This may sound something like, "It's a story about…um…a story…um…um…it's about…akidwhofliesakite… um…" This pattern may lead to misunderstandings and make others impatient—especially other children, because they don't have the broader, more mature perspective of an adult. Communication may be stymied as others either abandon the conversation or jump in and try to complete a child's statements.

Language Development

Children with ADHD process language differently than their peers. For starters, they have an increased risk for language delays (Sciberras et al. 2014). In addition, they're more likely to get off topic when speaking because of distractibility and related

ADHD symptoms. They frequently struggle to find the right words and put thoughts together quickly and linearly in conversation, leading to tangential comments. And even when they have a grasp of good grammar, they're more prone to errors as they compose sentences because of their planning difficulties.

Listening comprehension can also be impaired directly by ADHD, even in the absence of a specific language delay, because of difficulty processing rapidly spoken language. They have the capacity to understand, but because of their ADHD, they miss details. When listening, they may lose the thread of the conversation and therefore not register vital information. This can result in behavior that seems oppositional, but actually isn't, when requests aren't heard in the first place.

For children with ADHD, paying attention to a single exchange can be especially problematic in groups or noisy situations. Focusing on one person and transitioning attention between speakers is challenging for them. This has social implications and explains why some people with ADHD find it's easier to communicate one-on-one than in a group. For these reasons, children with ADHD may have particular difficulty in distracting classrooms with multiple activities occurring simultaneously, such as several adults leading separate lessons.

In addition, ADHD often makes it hard to manage large clumps of words all at once. While one eight-year-old may be able to hear and understand as many as twelve words without a pause, for an eight-year-old with ADHD seven or eight words might be the maximum (McInnes et al. 2003). With longer sentences, information starts to drop out. Of course, missing the ending greatly alters the meaning of a sentence like "You can go outside and play with your friends after your homework is done."

These issues aren't due to problems with the auditory system. The information is received, but executive function impairments cause it to be mismanaged. The brain manager is asleep on the job, jumbling the details of what's being said.

Pragmatic Language

Pragmatic language encompasses the social customs around spoken language and nonverbal communication, and core ADHD symptoms can undermine this aspect of communication. Behaviors such as blurting out answers, interrupting, talking excessively, and speaking too loudly break conventions around communication. Among people with ADHD, even those with advanced vocabularies and understanding for their age may experience pragmatic difficulties that get in the way of social fluency.

These difficulties are similar to, but not the same as, those found in children with autism. In autism, the underlying issue is that children don't intuitively grasp the social world, so by definition, they have pragmatic language delays. Unlike children with ADHD, they also have intrinsic developmental delays in a wide array of social and communication skills.

For children with ADHD, the ability to understand nonverbal language and social interactions typically remains intact. They recognize nonverbal communication for what it is and understand basic rules of communication such as "Wait for your turn to reply." However, due to distractibility, impulsiveness, or other executive function impairments, they may sometimes fail to follow those rules or to even notice social cues at all.

Keep Tally of Your Talking

According to psychologist John Gottman, in a healthy marriage, positive feedback significantly outweighs negative feedback (Gottman 2012). The same holds true for almost any relationship. But because children with ADHD require more redirection due to their executive function issues and ADHD-related behaviors, they often receive ongoing negative, corrective feedback, skewing the ratio toward the negative.

On a busy day as you're trying to get out the door, the entire focus may fall on redirection: "Hurry up, we're going to be late! Did you brush your teeth and put your clothes in the hamper? Where's your jacket? Stop hassling your sister. Quick! To the bus." During frustrating times, it's all too easy to focus only on what absolutely has to happen. And even the most patient and supportive parent has to coach a child with ADHD through the day, tipping the ratio of feedback toward the negative.

Correction isn't wrong and is frequently unavoidable, and empty praise doesn't carry much weight either. It therefore takes conscious effort to create balance by habitually noticing and praising even small moments of success. Most days you can find at least brief accomplishments, and your child will benefit from hearing about them: "Thank you for getting dressed right away." "Great job listening."

Throughout, it's helpful to come back to practicing mindfulness. Everyone's mind gets scattered. We all feel pulled in countless different directions. Negative experiences, such as arguments, often hold our attention long after they pass. When they take over, we can no longer clearly see what's happening in the moment. Mindfulness helps us notice and focus on the positive instead of getting trapped in negativity.

Actions Speak Louder Than Words: Helping Your Child with Communication Issues

As you begin to work on monitoring your communication style, you're probably eager to get started on helping your child with communication issues too. The following strategies can enhance or improve communication. Some are related to addressing your child's communication, and some will help you adapt your own communication style.

Seek out an evaluation. If you or someone working with your child has concerns about your child's capacities in any aspect of communication, seek out speech-language testing and then initiate any therapies indicated. Remember that in spite of common misperceptions, the term "auditory processing" refers to symptoms typically found with either learning disabilities or ADHD. Addressing these underlying disorders benefits children far more than auditory-based interventions.

Address pragmatic language concerns if your child is struggling socially. A behavioral plan alone may not be enough to ease your child's social struggles if his language skills are also impaired. The assistance of a speech-language therapist familiar with pragmatic language may be required.

Encourage language development. For a young child, engage in conversation often and emphasize books and reading together at home. "Educational" television and DVDs don't appear to improve language abilities (Christakis et al. 2009). Children learn best from engaged caretakers (DeLoache et al. 2010). You can also build skills by reframing what a young child says. For example, if a toddler with language delays points to a milk carton and says "Muh," you might respond with, "Would you like some milk?" If an older child tells a disjointed, rambling story about his day, you can lightly redirect him back to the original topic and help him expand his ideas: "So you had fun during recess today. Tell me more about how you play that game."

Wait until you have your child's full attention. Before making requests or starting conversations, make sure your child is listening. He's likely to miss important details if you speak while his attention is elsewhere. Help him transition his attention by using a brief marker, such as "Joseph, I have a question for you." If it's helpful, engage him physically by gently touching his shoulder or something similar. Once you have your child's attention, try to maintain eye contact.

Offer your child more time in conversation. If your child is struggling to pull his thoughts together, give him ample time to settle himself and organize his thoughts. Try not to speak until he's finished his turn. Resist the temptation to talk over your child or complete his statements.

Be clear and make sure your message is getting across. Enunciate clearly and use gestures, such as counting points on your fingers. Without judgment or condescending, rephrase or repeat yourself as needed. Consider having your child restate what he understood you to say.

Divide requests into shorter segments. Simplifying requests by asking that your child do only one step at a time improves his chances of understanding and complying. This makes it likelier that he'll succeed and creates an opportunity for targeted praise, which supports effective behavioral planning.

Consider any need for communication repair after difficult conversations. Effective communication doesn't require perfection. We all sometimes struggle to express ourselves or patiently listen. After any interaction, consider whether you need to clarify details, apologize, or tell your child you'd like to hear more. All are vital parts of effective communication.

Communication Repair

So you have a child whom you love without bounds, and yet sometimes he infuriates you. He wakes to read at five in the morning even though you know he would be happier with more sleep. You mostly manage to ignore his whining and tantrums, but they persist for months, always about the exact same things.

On and on it goes, and at some point you max out. You do exactly what you promised yourself you'd never do. You shut down, get angry, or just feel completely at a loss. You may then fall back on old, less effective communication habits, or even toss the entire idea of managing your child's ADHD right out the window.

What's the answer? There is no perfect, singular solution much of the time. The first step toward mending such situations, before addressing them with your child, is to check in with your own experience. Pause and let the situation de-escalate. Then take a moment to consider your child's perspective. Perhaps apologize and make amends if it's needed. And then set an intention, in words at first and afterward through your actions, to compromise and try something new in guiding your child forward.

The Communication Mirror

Children absorb more from their parents through what they observe than through what they hear. What skills do you want your child to develop for handling tense conversations? Through your actions, what would you like your child to discover about manners, listening, handling conflict, speaking respectfully, and everything else related to the complex world of communication?

Exercise: Focusing on Success in Communication

A classic Spanish proverb advises, "Before speaking, make certain your words will be an improvement on the silence." One way to follow this sage advice is to monitor for a short stretch of time how you habitually communicate with your child. This next exercise will help you do just that.

Over the next several days, observe how you communicate with your child, noticing both more effective and less effective communication patterns. Here are some examples of approaches that typically don't encourage successful communication. Attend to how often you communicate in these ways, and if you notice that you're about to do so, pause and consider taking a different approach:

- Starting to speak before your child finishes

- Finishing your child's statements

- Using overly long sentences (more than about ten words) without a pause

- Speaking without pausing to listen

- Giving instructions with multiple parts or asking questions with multiple parts

- Speaking to your child reactively, rather than intentionally

- Using barbed comments meant to correct your child: "For the thousandth time, get started on your homework!"

- Making hurtful, reactive comments that reflect your disappointment, frustration, or anger: "I can't take care of you forever."

At the same time, monitor how often you offer your child encouragement, and actively work toward increasing successful communication. Make an effort to point out and label what goes well when it happens, both verbally and with physical affection. Note these moments before your child has a chance to take off in another direction. Begin to focus on providing more positive feedback than negative every day, with upbeat statements along these lines:

- "Thank you for…"

- "Great job…"

- "I appreciate when…"

- "Nice job on…"

To increase your chances of success, spend some time coming up with positive comments that feel natural to you and list them here so they'll come to you more easily in the moment:

_____

_____

_____

_____

_____

_____

Mindfulness and Communication

As a reminder, being mindful doesn't mean having idyllic images of yourself that put you in a position to chronically fall short. Rather, by pausing and paying attention, you can identify personal traits you'd like to develop and habits you want to discourage. You can notice when you miss the mark and, without giving yourself a hard time, aim back toward your intentions.

Bringing mindfulness into communication starts with awareness and responsiveness. As you move out of autopilot, you can notice all the nuances of whatever is going on. Then you can pause briefly to settle your thoughts. That centered point can be challenging to maintain in the midst of an intense discussion, but it will help you stay in touch with your best intentions.

To be more genuinely responsive, you have to tune in to all the things you may be reacting to in the first place. You might discover a judgmental inner voice, find yourself lost in dense thoughts about the future or the past, or simply notice that you woke up in an awful mood that's darkening your outlook.

Gut reactions to even seemingly straightforward experiences in life often reflect layers of thoughts and emotions. So although you may be angry because your child hasn't done his homework, perhaps there are deeper layers of fear about what could happen five years from now if his academic performance doesn't improve. Or perhaps you struggled with homework yourself as a child, and that memory is coloring your present experience.

To support yourself in becoming more genuinely responsive, especially with your child, it's helpful to bring awareness to the many facets of your experience as you communicate, especially your thoughts, emotions, body language, and sensations, as outlined below.

Awareness of thoughts. As you enter a conversation with your child, you may have already decided how he'll react and what he'll say. You may make assumptions about his culpability based on what you've seen in the past, but maybe this time it isn't his fault. Nothing shuts down a conversation more quickly than an assumption of guilt, such as entering the room stating, "Out with it! You'd better have a good explanation for why you aren't doing your homework." You may be anticipating excuses and denials, yet perhaps this will be the time he charts a new path. Remember, thoughts are just thoughts, sometimes accurate, sometimes inaccurate. Fully listening requires setting aside judgments, presumptions, and assumptions and recognizing the other person's perspective, even when you disagree.

Awareness of emotions. Under stress, the brain's fear center takes over and shuts down flexible thinking and responding. Physical and mental reflexes take over. Being excessively angry, upset, anxious, or exhausted is likely to prevent a productive, intentional conversation. At these times, the best bet is to take a break and do what you can to ground yourself and allow for more skillful communication. Doing a brief mindfulness practice can be very helpful. But sometimes you won't have an opportunity to settle yourself before continuing. Mindfulness can help here as well: remain aware that you're rattled and not at your best.

Awareness of body language. Our bodies often disclose far more than the words we say. Any good poker player can tell you that facial expressions, mannerisms, and how people hold themselves reveal what they're thinking. When interacting with your child, monitor your facial expressions, how close you're standing, how you're holding your arms, and any other body language. Along similar lines, monitor what your tone of voice may be conveying.

Awareness of physical sensations. Also tune in to physical sensations. This may allow you to notice when an interaction is starting to go awry and redirect yourself. For example, if you pick up the vague nausea you feel when you're nervous, that may be the first sign that you're getting overwhelmed, and it may show up long before your conscious mind typically figures it out. By noticing your tense hands, furrowed brow, or whatever other warning flag has arisen, you can intervene early and break a cycle of reactivity.

Awareness of ADHD. Awareness of ADHD isn't technically a component of your inner experience, given that it's an awareness that is itself comprised of thoughts, emotions, and physical sensations. But in your efforts to communicate more effectively with your child, awareness of his ADHD can be quite useful. For example, distractibility, impulsiveness, interrupting, talking too loudly, or being overly talkative can all disrupt discussions. Recognizing them as ADHD symptoms may help reduce your frustration and reactivity and increase your ability to facilitate effective communication.

Q&A

Q: I find all this self-examination exhausting. Why would I want to pay attention all the time? Can't I be impulsive and have fun too?

A: One common trap in practicing mindfulness is taking an approach that's too intense. You may feel like you're picking over your experience instead of just living. That can be paralyzing and no more helpful than acting on your first impulse. Mindfulness practice is like tuning a stringed instrument: aim for attention that's neither too lax nor too tight. If you feel an overwhelming sense of effort, step back a little. In fact, practicing mindfulness can promote spontaneity—and fun—as you let go of old ways of seeing things, which frees you to try something new.

Exercise: Imagining Communication Advice to a Friend

This exercise, along with a related exercise that follows shortly, will help you refine your own communication style by imagining the advice you'd give to a friend who was facing a challenging conversation. For the first part of the exercise, read through the instructions, then put the book aside and do the practice.

To begin, sit quietly for a few minutes. Close your eyes or lower your gaze to the floor and observe your breathing as best you can. Whenever your mind wanders, return your attention to breathing.

Now imagine that you have a friend who works for an irrational boss. She has a meeting to resolve a problem at work. Your friend isn't responsible for her boss's volatile behavior. And yet among all the possibilities for what she might say or how she might conduct herself, some might make the conversation degenerate into a verbal brawl, others might lead to her slinking out of the room having gained nothing, and yet others might defuse the situation and keep the conversation on track. What advice would you offer to support her in managing the situation effectively? Consider all of these aspects of the situation:

- *How might she stand up for her convictions while keeping things on an even keel?*

- *What might help her stand up for her point of view?*

- *What might help keep the situation balanced and productive?*

- *How would she hold herself, and what tone of voice and language would she use?*

- *How might she approach the situation internally, and what thoughts might she use to guide herself?*

End this part of the exercise whenever you choose, taking a few more mindful breaths and then opening your eyes.

Now distill your advice to your friend in the space below. Later, you can reflect on these descriptions to establish intentions for your own communication patterns with your child.

Sounds, including tone of voice, rate of speaking, sentence length, and pauses to listen, as well as environmental distractions:

_____

_____

_____

Body language, including facial expressions and posture: _____

_____

_____

Physical sensations: _____

_____

_____

Emotional states before, during, and after the imagined interaction: _____

_____

_____

Thoughts and assumptions, including expectations prior to the interaction and rumination about it afterward:

_____

_____

_____

Using an ADHD Plan to Support Mindful Communication

Like most people, you probably have a vision of how you'd ideally manage confrontations, and you probably recognize the benefits of a measured, dispassionate approach. You may remember to pause and bring your intentions to mind. But what happens when, after pausing, you still find yourself in the midst of that challenging situation with no clear idea about what to do next?

It's hard to remain responsive when you don't have a solid plan for handling ADHD. You may eventually find yourself shouting, giving in, or whatever else you set out not to do. Identifying direct communication strategies to use with your child will make it easier to stick to your intentions. You need both mindfulness and a skillfully constructed plan.

During a calmer moment, with time to reflect, use the skills you'll continue to learn in this book to establish a new strategy. Come up with targeted solutions for the situations that trigger you most. Then, next time those situations arise, when you pause you'll have another option: *I feel like exploding, but instead I'll remind my child of the consequence for this behavior.* Then write that solution down and post it where it can serve as a reminder.

Over time, continue to monitor communications with your child. Use the STOP practice frequently, pausing and making a conscious effort to act and speak in accordance with your intentions. Use what you wrote in the exercise "Imagining Communication Advice to a Friend" to remind yourself of your intentions, perhaps posting it as a visible reminder as well.

Exercise: Observing Your Communication Style

This exercise is similar to "Imagining Communication Advice to a Friend," but in this case you'll imagine a conversation with your child.

As in the earlier exercise, start with a few moments of mindful breathing. Then bring a recent challenging conversation with your child to mind. Guide yourself through the various aspects of the interaction, including your thoughts, emotions, and physical sensations. End this part of the exercise whenever you choose, taking a few more mindful breaths.

Next, take time to write about the different aspects of the interaction outlined below:

Sounds, including tone of voice, rate of speaking, sentence length, and pauses to listen, as well as environmental distractions:

_____

_____

_____

Body language, including facial expressions and posture: _____

_____

_____

Physical sensations: _____

_____

_____

Emotional states before, during, and after the interaction:_____

_____

_____

Thoughts and assumptions, including expectations prior to the interaction and rumination about it afterward:

_____

_____

_____

Now compare what you've written here to what you wrote in the earlier exercise. How is it similar to the advice you'd give a friend? How is it different? Notice any tendency to judge yourself for having been "good" or "bad." Notice any sense of having let yourself or your child down. That's only your inner critic again.

Finally, based on what you've learned, set a new intention about how you'll communicate with your child. Moving forward, let go of expectations, follow your intentions, and allow each new conversation to open the door to more productive and supportive ways of communicating.

Action Plan: Practicing Mindful Communication

So much of how any conversation goes is steered by how each person conducts himself or herself. In even the tensest moment, you have an opportunity to de-escalate the situation by listening and expressing yourself in ways that make successful communication more likely. Even when your child seems to be intentionally oppositional, managing your side of the conversation well can set the stage for change. Here are some specific steps to take in that direction:

- ☐ Listen first. When you feel a serious conversation is needed, allow your child the opportunity to express his perspective first. Then, if you disagree, pause and explain why.

- ☐ Notice your expectations about how conversations with your child will go or assumptions about his thoughts, and set them aside while listening.

- ☐ Monitor your body language, posture, tone of voice, and facial expression and make sure they're in alignment with what you want to convey.

- ☐ Monitor your emotional state and its influence on the situation. If you're feeling strong emotions, consider taking a break or having the discussion at another time.

- ☐ Pause before and during speaking. Make sure your child is done speaking before you respond, and make sure you're being heard when it's your turn. Ask for repetition or rephrasing periodically if you are uncertain.

- ☐ Monitor yourself in any discussion by using the STOP or Fifteen Breaths practices. For challenging conversations, pause, take a few mindful breaths, and observe both before starting and periodically throughout. Then refocus on your intentions for communicating with your child.

- ☐ Continue your daily mindfulness practice, using both in-the-moment practices, such as STOP and Fifteen Breaths, and more formal practices, such as Awareness of the Breath or Mindful Eating.

Chapter 6

Emphasizing Success with Targeted Praise and Rewards

Read this chapter to...

- Develop a success-based approach to behavior management

- Create proactive, step-by-step measures to reinforce family-based behavioral plans

- Use mindfulness to augment positive behavioral supports

People often have the belief that happiness awaits them one day out in the future: *Once my job situation settles...*, *Once we can afford a new car...*, and even—or especially—*Once my child's ADHD is under control...* Meanwhile, life continues. What happens today when happiness is only a distant end point?

This kind of mismatch between beliefs about how life should be before you can be happy and how life actually is causes a lot of stress all on its own. In some ways, stress can be seen as what transpires when we've either gotten what we didn't want or didn't get what we did want. Something isn't how it "should" be, and something must be done about that.

Grasping on to how things should be will also impair your ability to create a successful behavioral plan for your child. Forgetfulness around homework provides a good example: *She's in high school, but she still isn't handing in her homework regularly. She should take more responsibility for herself and work harder. She should care more.* The situation aggravates you, your child's teachers, and even your child. Meanwhile, today, what would it feel like to let go of the belief that things shouldn't be like this? Forgetfulness is a specific ADHD symptom, albeit one that's frustrating and disruptive for everyone involved. Still, thinking things should be different won't change the situation; creating a new plan might.

Sometimes problems pass when we let go of "shoulds." Perhaps one day you stop cleaning up your daughter's disaster of a room and drop the topic. Both of you may find some immediate relief. And then, after the clutter accumulates for a few weeks, maybe she'll discover the benefits of tidying up once in a while. Sometimes by letting go you open the door to new solutions—and also relieve a lot of stress.

Letting go in this way doesn't mean becoming a doormat. It also doesn't mean viewing everything as great when it isn't. You'll still have things you want to work on. But you can aim to make creative and objective decisions even as you cultivate the ability to live comfortably with your current situation.

Your child's ADHD is a factor in your life; you can't change that. Balancing a healthy sense of what you can influence right now with acceptance of what you cannot increases the odds of finding ease for yourself and your child as you work toward solutions. It's also a vital step toward effective behavior management: seeing ADHD symptoms for what they are today, and then implementing targeted programs that both handle challenges and build skills for the future.

The first step is providing a healthy, supportive environment for your child, emphasizing positive feedback. Nearly every behavioral or educational program recognizes this vital starting point.

Empowering Parents and Children

When the day seems to be crumbling around you, your first thought may not be to focus on praise and rewards for your child—especially amidst her more challenging behaviors. Perhaps a playdate begins well, and then, out of the blue, your child pours an ice cream sundae down her supposed best friend's shirt. Or maybe the school year seemed to be off to a good start and then your child's teacher sends a terse e-mail asking where the last seven math sheets ended up. Or perhaps you realize that you no longer remember the color of the carpet that lies buried beneath the debris in your child's bedroom…and you may have dropped your gold earring in there yesterday.

Amidst these kinds of challenges, emphasizing your child's successes remains the foundation of a productive behavioral plan. Positive feedback is a key tool for modifying behavior. And while punishment may feel like a more concrete way to banish difficult behaviors (and may be necessary in particular situations), positive feedback is essential for fostering healthy relationships, resilience, motivation, and self-confidence in your child.

With ADHD, any behavioral plan starts with parents. Even though you may really wish your child would figure out what could benefit her, the solutions you devise and implement will be most effective. And while it may seem that children should work on skills on their own, individual behavioral interventions for children with ADHD are most effective for issues that co-occur with it, such as anxiety and self-esteem (MTA Cooperative Group 1999). As children get older, individual therapy can also guide them toward managing their own ADHD. For everything else, parents are far more likely to hold on to successful plans and sustain them over time, even when day-to-day results are hard to detect.

Q&A

Q: How can I create plans for one child with ADHD when I have other kids living at home?

A: Everything that supports children with ADHD helps all children, and any concept related to ADHD can be adapted to help an entire household. Instead of having two styles of parenting or multiple behavioral systems, use the same approach for everyone.

Getting Started with Behavioral Training

As discussed, because ADHD involves difficulties with executive function skills, children with ADHD require a lot of correction and redirection throughout the day. Therefore, most children with ADHD end up receiving an inordinate amount of negative feedback. The redirection can't be dropped outright; you have to get your child to school on time and help her accomplish basic daily tasks.

Shifting the balance toward positive feedback requires focused, proactive effort. Yet this can be challenging, as children with ADHD are slower to respond, harder to motivate, and find routines difficult. However, putting in the effort will make your life easier over time. It's also important for your child's well-being. To that end, this chapter covers positive reinforcement and specific techniques for emphasizing success and providing positive feedback even while addressing challenging behaviors. (Chapter 7 addresses setting limits skillfully.) The three key components of positive reinforcement are as follows:

- Spending time together consistently

- Offering targeted praise

- Using defined rewards

Stick with these basics through thick and thin, even when discipline is required. Take time with each component to establish it before moving on to the next. In this way, you can build a platform of success that will empower both you and your child.

Give Your Child Your Full Attention Once a Day

As you've probably seen for yourself, problematic behaviors often start as a call for attention. Children depend on quality time with their parents, even when this isn't apparent from what they do or say. Spending quality time together won't change all of your child's difficult behaviors on its own, but it will establish a solid foundation for your relationship.

Between all the demands of everyday life, it can be easy to lose touch with family time. Yet even something as straightforward as eating meals together as a family has been correlated with childhood well-being (Fiese and Schwartz 2008). Periodically take some time to reexamine your family schedule and reprioritize based on what you value.

As part of that, commit to giving each of your children your full attention once a day, keeping these tips in mind:

- Schedule the time you'll spend together and stick to it. You may need to set different times for different days, depending on everyone's schedule. You may instead need to rotate days between your children, if you have more than one. If you work during the week, be sure to protect weekend time with your family.

- Schedule at least fifteen minutes of together time.

- During this time, focus fully on your child as best you can.

- During your scheduled time together, turn off your smartphone and the TV and follow your child's lead, wherever she may go. Let your child pick the activity (as long as it doesn't violate household rules). That said, encourage her to choose an activity that involves both of you, rather than you simply watching her do something on her own, like play a favorite solo game.

Pride in Play

Following a child's lead doesn't always feel easy or straightforward. One behavioral program, parent-child interaction therapy (Eyberg and Funderburk 2011), suggests the following PRIDE acronym for you to guide yourself when you feel less than engaged:

P = Praise: Encourage appropriate behaviors by giving immediate feedback: "Great job asking politely!"

R = Reflect: Repeat back and provide commentary on what your child says and does: "You played freeze tag with Josephine? That sounds fun."

I = Imitate: Copy your child when she plays. If she imagines her dolls taking the bus to school, participate and follow along. If she draws pictures, draw your own.

D = Describe: Show interest and expand your child's vocabulary by describing what you see. "Isabella is on the swing? Who is she playing with today?"

E = Enjoy: Display enthusiasm about whatever your child is saying and doing while you play together.

Offer Targeted Praise

In daily life with your child, make a concerted effort to give positive feedback each time you observe a behavior you want to encourage. Children are motivated by positive comments, although this isn't always evident on the surface. Even a sullen teenager will benefit from hearing directly that she's met your approval.

In addition to giving positive feedback more generally, you can use praise to selectively reinforce specific habits and behaviors. Here are some pointers on how to do so.

Choose the behavior you most want to cultivate. You can promote a particular behavior by commenting on it: "Look at that! You're ready for the bus five minutes early. That's awesome!"

Point out success before your child has a chance to make a mistake. Most children can shift from desirable to undesirable behavior in a flash. When you notice that your child has succeeded in a targeted behavior, let her know right away, before she has a chance to get off track: when you see appropriate play with a sibling (before the bickering), when she starts her homework (but isn't yet complaining), and so on.

Value activities your child enjoys and feels successful in. ADHD often undermines social skills and academic performance, so help your child develop interests that allow her to experience success elsewhere. Show her that you value whatever interests her, from art to sports and from writing to dance.

Avoid empty praise. Targeted praise emphasizes specific behaviors you want to cultivate. Empty praise, on the other hand, is nonspecific positive feedback or praise for something beyond your child's control. Some researchers (Mueller and Dweck 1998) believe empty praise can undermine long-term motivation, particularly when emphasizing fixed traits ("You're so clever") over effort ("You must have tried really hard").

Celebrate effort. Your child's long-term motivation will improve most if you praise perseverance and hard work. In contrast, a focus on more specific outcomes, such as grades or winning, can undermine long-term effort and also frustrate a child with ADHD, whose symptoms often get in the way. Plus, targeting effort rather than specific achievements can increase your opportunities to offer praise: "Nice race—you wouldn't have tripped if you hadn't been running so hard."

Mindfulness makes it easier to provide targeted praise, as it can help you avoid the negativity bias that's common in the human brain. Our minds hold on to whatever seems dangerous or in need of fixing, a bias that persists throughout life. Problematic behaviors grab our attention. Successful behaviors frequently don't; they just happen.

During family time, notice when you're caught up in mental detritus or just the business of family life, and then guide yourself back to the moment. It often requires conscious effort to remember to both notice and comment on the little stuff that doesn't otherwise call for your attention. Use your mindfulness practice to help you stay on track in pointing out specific behaviors you're trying to encourage.

Practice: Keeping a Gratitude Journal

The human brain is wired for self-protection and has a hard time letting go of anything that seems off or potentially dangerous. It's an important reflex that protects us from harm. Over the course of your day, countless things happen. Most probably go well, but the difficult or unpleasant moments tend to stand out and seem most important. Countering this tendency can go a long way toward increasing your happiness and well-being.

One way to do this is to keep a gratitude journal. At the end of the day, reflect on and briefly record what you're thankful for or what has gone well. The format doesn't matter; you can use a notebook or record your thoughts on your smartphone. This approach can also support you in giving your child positive feedback if you specifically include things you are grateful for in your child.

Establish a Reward System

When parents reward the *opposite* of problem behaviors, children experience positive feedback and at the same time avoid behaviors that could lead to punishment. Using this core principle of behavioral modification, you can reinforce behaviors you want to encourage, no matter what your child's age. It also provides an opportunity to work collaboratively with your child to achieve success.

Reward systems are not just useful for ending difficult behaviors. They can also encourage compliance with routines and ease transitions, which are often a struggle for children with ADHD: "Come on, get into bed quickly. You're so close to earning your new doll!" When setting up rewards, also build in any needed adjustments to your child's attitude when performing tasks. For example, she might earn a point for completing her homework, but only if she does so without excessive hysterics.

Parents of children with ADHD often (and understandably) give up on reward systems early on, thinking the system doesn't seem to work or doesn't work quickly enough. There is also often an insidious belief that children should be more intrinsically self-motivated. In addition, the energy required to sustain the plan can seem daunting. And yet in spite of these common hurdles, this type of behavioral plan can resolve many household tensions and eradicate many disruptive behaviors.

Exercise: Establishing a Reward System

This exercise will guide you through all of the steps of creating an effective reward system. Take as much time as needed with each step, and remain patient with yourself and your child as you implement your new plan and then make any needed adjustments.

Start with Behavioral Triage

You can't expect to overcome all problematic behaviors at once. Taking on too many things simultaneously will undermine effective planning. It's overwhelming for both parents and children, and also difficult to maintain because it's too complex: "Make your bed, be nice to your sister, and make sure you've done your homework, and then you'll earn a point for each one. Once you get two hundred points, you earn a prize." Instead, keep it simple and sustain a steady march forward by adding new items over time.

For your initial reward system, choose one or two of the behaviors that are currently most problematic and write them here:

1. _____

2. _____

For anything you aren't actively addressing right now, set it aside as much as possible to ease the sense of wrestling. If you aren't actively working on something, it isn't likely to change rapidly, but you will get to it when it's time. In fact, simply ignoring difficult behaviors may improve them, as discussed in chapter 7.

Identify the Opposite of Difficult Behaviors

Define an appropriate behavior that's the flip side of the one you'd like to eliminate. This will be the targeted behavior. For example, to decrease whining, you might choose "speaking politely," or if your child stuffs her mouth when eating, you could reward polite table manners. This approach allows your child to experience success instead of failure.

Write the opposite, targeted behaviors here:

1. _____

2. _____

Emphasize Sustainable Small Steps Toward Change

If your child is to buy into the reward system, she must be able to earn points most of the time. If you set the bar too high at the outset, she won't experience success and will lose interest or motivation. Giving points when your child hasn't really earned them also undermines the system. So guide her behavior forward by defining manageable, incremental steps toward larger goals.

For example, if your child hits others when angry and also talks back, start by rewarding "keeping your hands to yourself all day [or for a certain part of the day]." Once that resolves, however long it takes, switch to giving points for speaking appropriately.

Write the first step in achieving each targeted behavior here:

1. _____

2. _____

Consider Breaking the Day into Smaller Parts

Another way to create more opportunities for success is to divide up the day. For example, your child can earn a point for appropriate behavior before school and another for appropriate behavior after school. This way, if she makes a mistake in the first part of the day, she can still earn a reward later that day.

In the space below, write any divisions for earning rewards, such as before school or before lunch:

Targeted behavior 1

Division 1. _____

Division 2. _____

Division 3. _____

Targeted behavior 2

Division 1. _____

Division 2. _____

Division 3. _____

Decide upon a Reward

The type of reward depends on your child and her age. Young children with ADHD need immediate feedback. If you give a young child a sticker for each success, that may be sufficient. Have an older child earn points or tokens toward a more major reward or prize.

To make sure rewards will be compelling for your child, consider involving her in selecting them. Typical rewards include small toys (consider a visit to a dollar store), movie night with a friend, dinner at a restaurant your child enjoys, accessories for a favorite toy, video games or accessories, clothing, or extra screen time. Make sure the reward is manageable in terms of cost and how much time it's likely to take your child to earn it (more on this shortly).

Once you've selected a reward, write it here:

_____

Establish How Many Points Are Needed for the Reward

Decide how long you want it to take for your child to earn the reward, keeping in mind both your child's age and the size of what she'll earn. A child in early elementary school would ideally earn a small reward every week or two. By high school, small rewards can occur weekly or you can aim for a more significant one every month or two.

Keep the size of the reward in mind too. Don't overreach. If you choose something epic, like a new computer, you may get great compliance. But that makes it hard to offer an equally motivating reward next time. Choose rewards large enough to hold your child's interest, but modest enough that you can offer them repeatedly.

Calculate the points needed based on the minimum number of days it could take to earn the prize. For example, if you want at least two weeks between rewards and your child can earn 2 points each day, 28 points should be required for the reward.

Don't tie rewards to fixed amounts of time: "If you earn a point for getting dressed every day this week, you get to do something special this weekend." That type of plan requires unerring success. If your child doesn't earn a point on Monday, the system will have no value to her for the rest of the week. Instead, set up the plan so that whenever she earns a certain number of points, she gets to do something special.

Once you've decided how many points are required to earn the reward, write the number here:

_____

Create a Visual Record of Your Child's Progress

To help your child see her progress, use sticker charts, fill a jar with tokens, keep a checklist, or use whatever works to draw attention to the plan. A simple chart is provided here (and available for download), but you may need to set up your own depending on how many behaviors you're targeting and how you're dividing the day. In the appropriate boxes, record the number of points earned or use stickers to represent the points.

You can also find many visually exciting reward charts, appropriate to different ages, on the Internet. Whatever you use, post it prominently so your child can watch her progress. If your child doesn't find the plan interesting at first, try making the chart itself more engaging, for example, filling in parts of a picture until it's complete. A visual reminder of the reward can also be very motivating, so consider posting a photo of it or having it in sight but out of reach.

Behavioral goal:		
Start date:		
Day	Morning	Afternoon
Monday		
Tuesday		
Wednesday		
Thursday		
Friday		
Saturday		
Sunday		

Aim for Consistency

A reward system relies on ongoing targeted feedback. One common breakdown in busy families is that parents lose track of recording daily events and counting points. Collaborate with your partner or another adult to remember the plan, or set up a reminder on your phone, having it pop up toward the end the day. Also encourage your child to remind you. Keep the chart posted in a prominent place, and get your child involved in monitoring her progress so everyone develops a habit of noticing progress and reviewing the plan regularly.

Keep the System Compelling for Your Child

Children with ADHD get bored more easily than their peers, so change up the system from time to time. Your child may even lose sight of how much she'd love a particular reward. If she becomes disinterested, step back, let go of the old plan, and try something new.

Also vary your rewards. Younger children, up through early elementary school, may need nothing more than flashier stickers or new ones tied to a current movie or game. For older children, switch up the type of reward and time frame: small toys for short-term rewards versus larger items for long-term rewards, material objects versus one-time special events, and so on.

Supporting Reward Systems

As with much of parenting, positive feedback and logical reward plans take a lot of effort to maintain. They make sense on paper. You set a wholehearted intention. And then life gets in the way. Patiently remind yourself that you don't have to be perfect, only persistent. Also consider working with an ADHD professional to brainstorm and receive guidance. Reaching out for advice when things get challenging is a sign of confidence and strength, not failure. If behavioral systems don't seem effective, consider working with a psychologist or other specialist to problem solve and refine your approach.

Bringing Mindfulness to Praise and Rewards

It's not easy to put aside all the ADHD-related issues that worry or annoy you day to day. You have a long list of behavioral concerns, and at this point you may only be up to addressing item number two. Meanwhile, six others are getting under your skin on a daily basis. Your frustration and desire for change are real. But until you've solved whatever your current behavioral plan addresses, other stressful behaviors may persist.

When you notice yourself ruminating or fretting, as you probably will, consider the Fifteen Breaths practice. No matter how busy life gets, you have time for fifteen breaths. Acknowledge whatever is going on, then gently guide your mind away from all the sticky, negative thoughts for a moment. You can't make them go away. You can't fix the problem right now. So instead, practice letting go briefly, allowing thoughts to exist without fueling the fire.

Remind yourself that you're working on the most disruptive problems first. Those are the priority for the moment. You'll get to the rest of the list later. For a few seconds, choose not to wrestle with your discomfort or fall into habits of rumination, lashing out, shutting down or whatever else you tend to do when under stress.

Pause for a moment to focus on your immediate physical experience. You are here. The past is gone and the future has yet to unfold. Notice whatever distracts you from your larger intentions around praise and rewards and then return to your intentions again and again.

Cut Yourself Some Slack

When obstacles arise, the intense, ongoing commentary of the inner critic can make us feel inadequate and cause us to become defensive or aggressive, or to shut down. Caught up in these inner battles, we may lose touch with our intentions and what we wish for our children.

Psychologist Kristin Neff, PhD, has extensively studied what happens when we forget to extend the same compassion to ourselves as we do to others. Neff defines self-compassion as "being kind and understanding toward oneself in instances of pain or failure rather than being harshly self-critical; perceiving one's experiences as part of the larger human experience rather than seeing them as isolating; and holding painful thoughts and feelings in mindful awareness rather than over-identifying with them" (2003, 23). Research has linked self-compassion to everything from decreased anxiety when under threat to overall well-being (Neff 2009).

Self-compassion isn't the same as self-indulgence or self-pity. It doesn't mean seeing yourself as perfect. Like everyone else, you're flawed and trying your best. Self-compassion allows you to accept that less-than-perfect state even while aiming to improve.

Developing a sense of compassion for yourself requires developing a new relationship with your inner critic. If you try to suppress your inner critic, it may push back and become more powerful. It isn't a logical voice, so trying to rationalize with it won't work. An alternative approach is to simply label its message: "There's my distaste for being wrong." Then practice noticing that type of thought without getting as caught up in it. It may still be there, but you don't have to believe it.

You can create some space between you and your inner critic by reminding yourself that what it says isn't fact—it's just a thought. If you have something to make amends for, you can, and if there's something you want to work on, you should. Resolving to improve yourself is beneficial, but pervasive self-judgment isn't.

This is something you do not only for yourself, but also because it affects how you interact with others. Self-compassion promotes healthy relationships (Neff and Beretvas 2012). So when you notice your inner critic rattling on, take a mental step back: *Thanks for the opinion, but I've got this.* Instead of collapsing under the weight of self-criticism, cultivate another view: *I yell more than I'd like, but a lot less than I used to.* When you don't add fuel to its fire, your inner critic's voice will grow weaker and weaker.

For any challenge in life, notice where self-judgment exacerbates your emotional state. What's the actual issue, and how does self-criticism relate? Even when you can't yet define a next step forward, what might you do for yourself in the meantime? You may find that taking your inner critic less seriously not only makes you feel more at ease in the moment, but also makes it a lot more likely that your next decision reflects your intentions.

Exercise: Give Yourself a Real Break

The following exercise from Kristin Neff (http://www.centerformsc.org) can help you shift away from the overly harsh perspective you might otherwise take with yourself:

1. Take some time to reflect on something that makes you feel bad about yourself, whether a physical attribute, something about your personality, or certain ways of behaving or reacting. Then write a description of that quality.

2. Write the emotions you feel about that aspect of yourself.

3. Now picture a friend, real or imagined, who accepts you unconditionally—someone who understands and values the whole of who you are and knows your life history.

4. Write a letter to yourself from your friend's perspective, offering yourself compassion about this perceived problem.

5. Return to the letter as often as needed to remind you to allow yourself the same leniency a close friend would extend.

Action Plan: Accentuating the Positive with Behavioral Planning

Compassionate and effective behavior management begins with an emphasis on success, through targeted praise and rewards. Shifting your household dynamic to emphasize positive feedback can be challenging, but the tools and techniques in this chapter will help you get there. Here are the key action items:

☐ Schedule time with your child. Write your scheduled times here:

_____

_____

_____

☐ Offer targeted praise, and watch out for times that you get so caught up in thoughts or emotions that you miss opportunities to give positive feedback. Write the current behaviors for targeted praise here:

_____

_____

☐ Create a reward chart and make sure it includes an achievable behavior, an appropriate reward, and the number of points required to earn the reward.

☐ Continue to practice mindfulness daily, both formally, as a planned activity, and informally in the moment, especially when you're stressed or unsettled. Also assess your practice. How has it been going? Do you need to make any adjustments?

☐ Your updated plan for a daily formal mindfulness practice:

_____

_____

_____

☐ Your updated plan for practicing mindfulness informally, in everyday activities:

_____

_____

_____

☐ Recommit to taking care of yourself. Amidst the ongoing demands of daily life and everything you're learning and working on with this book, your self-care may be getting short shrift. Identify a few nurturing activities to prioritize and write them here:

_____

_____

_____

Chapter 7

Addressing Challenging Behaviors

Read this chapter to...

- Understand that setting and upholding limits is both vital and uniquely challenging when parenting a child with ADHD

- Utilize other behavior management techniques that decrease problem behaviors, such as avoiding behavioral triggers, planned ignoring, and allowing your child to experience the natural consequences of certain behaviors

- Optimize behavior management, set limits, and enforce them calmly and consistently

L imits are a large part of why kids need parents. If children knew how to behave in public, eat balanced diets, pick clothes that make sense for the weather, treat their friends well, manage time, handle responsibilities, and live a healthy lifestyle from the start, we could get them an apartment when they're in kindergarten and leave them to it. Limits ready children for the road ahead.

Allowing your child to experience some frustration within a supportive, safe environment furthers his development. Commonsense, old-fashioned parenting clichés have roots in reality. Life isn't always fair, and you can't have something just because your friend has one. By establishing limits, whether around video games, nutrition, or treating others respectfully, you help your child learn to self-regulate, building executive function and moving down a path to greater independence.

Of course, kids resist, often quite resourcefully, which makes it hard for parents to hold firm. Perhaps you want your child to be happy right now, so you lose touch with your long-term planning and relent. At times, you may be too run-down to hold the line. Maybe your neighbors set different standards for their children, and you worry that they'll judge you for your approach or that your kids will think you're unfair. Even when your logical brain knows better, it can be tempting to give in.

Yet it is entirely possible to acknowledge how frustrated your child feels while still sticking to limits you've set: "I'm sorry it makes you upset, but you can't watch the entire *Lord of the Rings* trilogy tonight. We can talk about it when you've calmed down." Continue to balance struggles over limits with positive feedback, such as praise and rewards. Use humor, diversions, and distractions to ease the situation when you're able. Offer discussion and choices when appropriate, all the while firmly remaining in your role as a parent.

A Foundation for Setting Limits

Staying firm when your child is pushing back depends on your state of mind. A crucial way of maintaining balance around limits is to value and build your own strength and equanimity. Taking the time to care for yourself will support consistent parenting.

Left unattended, stress builds on itself. Our minds become busier and busier, our thoughts more intense and unclear. As discussed, thoughts trigger feelings, feelings trigger thoughts, and how you feel physically leads to other thoughts and emotions, creating a cycle that can undermine your capacity to be at your best.

When you recognize a thought as a thought, sometimes you can choose to let it slide: *I'm worried about meeting with my child's teacher next week, but there's nothing I can do about it in this moment. I might as well enjoy playing together for now.*

Likewise, recognizing a mood as a mood opens the door to responding and taking positive action rather than reacting. If you're tired, overcaffeinated, or under the weather, your mood may plummet. Then you may blame your spouse, your job, or the guy behind the coffee counter who seems to be moving too slow. Noticing that, you might redirect yourself: *I'm in a bad mood. Maybe a run would help. In the meantime, I'd better monitor how I speak.*

Sometimes you may notice physical tension before you become consciously aware that you're upset. For example, tightness in your face or a queasy stomach may be a signal that you're angry or anxious. When you notice these physiological warning signs early, you can guide yourself back to your intentions far more easily.

Instead of scrambling for a sense of calm when you most need it, continue to practice mindfulness to strengthen your awareness and responsiveness. As you pay more attention to the different strands of your experience, they'll have less influence on your actions at an unconscious level. You may notice the difference between stressful thoughts and feelings and your immediate reality more often. With practice, you'll create a stable platform of mindfulness that you can more easily access in difficult moments.

Behavioral Basics for Ending Challenging Behaviors

From impulse control to emotion regulation to anticipating the consequences of their actions, children with ADHD lag years behind their peers. Even when they understand rules, they don't always follow them. Delayed executive function makes it difficult for them to tolerate frustration and decreases their overall self-regulation. All of this makes it even more difficult for parents to uphold limits. It also means limits may not have as immediate an effect on the behavior of a child with ADHD.

In spite of these challenges, having consistent boundaries and limits will support your child in overcoming the effects of ADHD. As you begin to set limits and confront these difficulties, keep these important guidelines in mind:

- Kids want to succeed, however it appears from the outside. And given the right tools, they will.

- Executive function issues get in the way, so you need to create solutions that address these issues first.

- Adults drive behavioral change in children with ADHD.

As outlined in chapter 6, it's important to start with praise and rewards for targeted behaviors—desirable behaviors that are the opposite of your child's difficult ones. In fact, a warm and supportive environment is required to effectively implement limits (Drayton et al. 2014). There are also various ways to address behavior without setting limits, such as eliminating underlying causes, offering your child a new way to manage himself, ignoring certain problem behaviors, or allowing your child to experience the natural consequences of a behavior. So before we turn to the topic of setting limits, let's look at these alternatives.

Externalize the System

Any behavior that occurs occurs for a reason: desire for an object or someone's attention, to resolve an emotional state like anger or frustration, or countless other causes. With ADHD, a common trigger is when expectations exceed a child's current ability. Avoidance, frustration, and other problematic reactions arise when children face situations that require executive function skills they don't have. They push back, shut down, act out, or simply collapse emotionally.

You can use the tools in chapter 4 (in the Executive Function Management Tool Kit) to make tasks more approachable for your child. When you adjust your own actions or the environment to match your child's skills, many challenging situations will resolve. For example, tantrums and avoidance around homework can be addressed by modifying assignments or assisting with time management. Making situations and tasks more manageable eliminates the behaviors that crop up when children feel overwhelmed.

Avoid Behavioral Triggers

When a particular environment consistently leads to behavioral problems, consider avoiding that situation if possible. For example, if your child gets overstimulated in the supermarket, running around and grabbing exciting items off the shelves, one solution is to not bring him to the store. This isn't giving up. Over time, you can teach him appropriate behaviors. But in the meanwhile, avoiding the environment may be the wisest and most viable path. Of course, avoiding troublesome environments isn't always possible, so this chapter later covers behavior management outside the home.

Teach New Behaviors

An urge or emotion leads to any behavior, often a desire to have something or to relieve discomfort. For your child, simply stopping what he's doing is harder than redirecting the urge elsewhere. As an example, "Go to your room when you start to get frustrated" is much more achievable than "Never, ever throw a tantrum again." Through discussion, targeted praise, and rewards, you can work with your child to define new, healthier behaviors to replace problematic ones.

Planned Ignoring

Children's behaviors often derive from a desire to either grab others' attention or change people's minds. To a child, even negative attention from an adult may feel better than nothing. Therefore, if you don't respond at all, some behaviors may resolve on their own, whereas punishment or too much discussion may actually perpetuate them.

When your child is acting out, making a conscious choice to experience internal angst and not respond outwardly takes mindfulness and significant effort, but the results are worth it. When your bile rises and a cloud impairs your vision, you can focus your attention on breathing and choose to continue as if nothing is happening. Another option is to calmly state your intention ("I'm going to wait until you're settled") and then move on.

This approach is especially effective with tantrums. In the face of unremitting screaming, parents understandably give in to demands: "Fine. Go watch television. Just quiet down!" Children are quick learners, so that outcome reinforces the inappropriate behavior as useful. Though they were chastised, they still received what they wanted. Rendering the behavior useless by ignoring it makes it less likely to recur.

Coordinate with all caregivers to decide when ignoring a behavior is best. You can even pick what to say ahead of time: "I'm sorry you're upset. We can talk again when you're calm. You can kick and scream, but you're not getting anything that way." You might record your strategy and post it somewhere prominent (but don't post it publicly if that might upset your child).

Be aware that with any change in your approach, your child's behaviors may actually intensify for several days or weeks. If planned ignoring (or natural consequences, discussed below) leads to ongoing escalation, another approach may be needed. But quite often it does gradually improve behavior.

Let Your Child Learn from Natural Consequences

Children can also learn from being allowed to make a mistake and experience the outcome. Of course, you wouldn't use this approach in situations where your child's safety is at risk, only when the stakes are low. So instead of stepping in to redirect your child, you may choose to let him persist in his behavior and experience what happens. For example, if your child refuses to put on a jacket, let him go outside and get cold for a few minutes. If he won't stop goofing around, let him miss the beginning of a TV show he likes.

To use this approach well, you have to be aware of your child's ADHD-related limitations. Natural consequences only work when a child has the underlying ability to manage the situation or behavior. For example, with symptoms such as fidgeting, impulsiveness, or forgetfulness, natural consequences won't have much lasting effect. Building your child's skills and externalizing the system will be more beneficial.

So when natural consequences don't work, reevaluate your assumptions. As discussed, if your child habitually doesn't hand in his homework, it probably isn't under his control. You might think poor grades would be a natural consequence he could learn from, but the fact is, he is currently unable to remember to hand in his homework. Instead, you need to compensate for his ADHD symptom by helping him remember.

Distinguishing ADHD from Oppositional Defiant Disorder

People often wonder if their child with ADHD also has oppositional defiant disorder (ODD), a condition in which volitional oppositional behavior is an inherent trait. In reality, most children perceived as oppositional aren't *intentionally* difficult.

ADHD symptoms often mimic volitional behaviors. Messing up because of poor task management doesn't reflect any deeper intent, nor does reactively lashing out when asked to stop playing. Generally speaking, when children are given the tools to succeed, their behavior improves.

Further, a label of "oppositional defiant disorder" doesn't open the door to new solutions. A child acts in a particular way, and his parents have various options for addressing that behavior, regardless of the label. The diagnosis only adds an implication that the child has chosen to be defiant. That's possible, but we can give children the benefit of the doubt by starting from the assumption that executive function issues underlie their behavior.

A Key Tool in Setting Limits: Time-Outs

For limits to be effective, you need tools that encourage compliance. Yelling isn't useful in the long haul and mostly teaches kids to yell back. You can't take away privileges indefinitely. Discussion and explanation are useful, but they aren't discipline. Hitting your child is obviously inappropriate. You need a way to discourage problem behaviors—something to back up saying no.

Time-outs are currently the most proven technique for this purpose (Drayton et al. 2014). When used diligently, they allow you to dispassionately and directly enforce limits. Here's the basic procedure:

1. Establish a safe, quiet location for time-outs, such as a stair or chair away from household activity. Once time-outs have become familiar to both you and your child, you can also use them outside the home in some situations—although, of course, more direct supervision will be required to ensure your child's safety.

2. Set a timer for one minute per year of age. A three-year-old gets a three minute time-out, a ten-year-old ten minutes, and so on. You might round down, given

that your child has ADHD. Also note that some research indicates that four to five minutes will suffice regardless of age (Drayton et al. 2014).

3. When you see the behavior you want to eliminate, offer one warning, then begin a countdown to three: "If you don't stop, you'll get a time-out. I'm going to count to three. One…" The intention is for both you and your child to settle yourselves so the fight-or-flight response will shut down. Of course, if a behavior crosses a clear line and you don't have a chance to give a warning, skip the counting: "No hitting. You're in time-out right now."

4. Count slowly. If you reach three, time-out begins.

5. Don't start the timer until your child sits quietly. Let him know that if he leaves time-out or makes a fuss, you'll reset the timer. If he needs to correct something, like pick up a mess or apologize to someone, require him to do that when time-out is over.

6. Avoid discussion during counting and the time-out itself. In the midst of the tension, your voice will frequently trigger a stress response for your child once again, even when you're trying to offer a break. For this reason, statements like "Please settle down," "You don't want a time-out," or "I'm on two, now two and half," won't typically calm your child.

If your child resists time-outs, stand firm. You may have a week (or several) of extended, twenty-minute time-outs as you repeatedly reset the timer while waiting for compliance. But once you get past that, you'll have a vital tool for enforcing limits. Remember to keep emphasizing the positive, offering targeted praise for good behavior as you wait for time-outs to become effective.

As for yourself, you can use your child's time-outs for a brief mindfulness practice. Focus on your breath or physical sensations, or do another practice that you find useful so you're more settled when it's time to interact with your child again.

Redirecting Behavior by Setting Limits

Being more mindful doesn't mean being so calm and good-natured that you guide your child's behavior like Mary Poppins, with sweetness, song, and sleight of hand. Seeing things as they are includes recognizing that children sometimes require a firm stand from parents.

As mentioned, behavior occurs for a reason (*I want it, I'm angry, I'm craving attention*). What happens immediately after the behavior either reinforces it or discourages it from happening again. Positive outcomes—whether your child gets what he wants or grabs your attention—reinforce the behavior. Negative outcomes don't.

Young children learn best from these immediate consequences because, for them, "now" is not yet connected with "later." They don't really get the concept behind "If you eat all that ice cream, you won't be hungry for dinner." The ability to defer acting on an urge, thought, or emotion relies on self-regulatory skills that they haven't yet acquired.

Because of this perspective, delayed punishments are less effective. Statements such as "No computer this weekend" or "When your dad gets home…" seldom modify behavior much in younger children. Even when children seem remorseful, they don't necessarily connect that experience to their choices. With ADHD, this gap can persist across childhood.

Discussion alone, such as trying to explain why something is wrong or convince a child to make better choices, doesn't usually lead to behavioral change, but it does have value for creating context and clarifying your perspective. After discipline of some kind, it provides an explanation for your actions. Yet even with adolescents, who require more independence and collaboration, change is most likely with traditional behavior management.

Setting clear limits and sticking to them doesn't mean being cold or overly strict or demanding. Even while standing firm, you can bring lightness, humor, or whatever fits to your parenting style. Emphasize giving your child choices and freedom to explore whenever possible while still upholding key limits.

Setting Limits for Behavior at Home

You will most effectively set limits if you have a clear view of your child's capacities and how ADHD impacts them. As consistency is also crucial, continue to take time to care for yourself. When things get rough, don't beat yourself up; come back to your intentions and try again.

Prioritize

If you set limits for everything all the time, your child will suffer, and you'll probably end up exhausted and unhappy yourself. Keep behavioral triage in mind and work on just one or two of the most disruptive behaviors at a time. For behaviors that aren't up for change right now, perhaps see if planned ignoring gets you anywhere.

Stay Strong but Calm

Use time-outs as a dispassionate tool to prevent yelling, complaining, and escalation. Counting to three allows both you and your child to bring things down a notch.

Make Clear, Unambiguous Statements

As best you can, only make specific requests if you intend to follow through. If you say "Clear the table now" and then do it yourself when your child leaves, you've reinforced noncompliance. If you mean "I'd like it if you'd clear the table, but it's okay if you don't want to," say that instead.

Encourage conversation, freedom, and fun, but be clear and concise about limits: "It's bedtime and you need to go upstairs." Don't plead. Don't offer multiple reminders and then impose a limit when frustrated. Also monitor whether you sometimes ask questions when you mean to make a statement, such as "Don't you want to put your homework in your backpack now?" If you mean "Your homework needs to be in your backpack before you go play," say it.

Aim for Consistency

If the consequence for not observing a limit is a time-out, then once you've counted to three, start a time-out, without shouting or further discussion. Kids quickly learn to push back if you give in too often. You say, "No more video game time." He pushes back. You say no. He throws a tantrum. You walk away. He follows, whining. You need to make dinner, so you say, "Fine, a half hour more." What lesson has he learned?

Offer Choices Often, but Only When You Mean It

Involve children in problem solving, scheduling, and decisions whenever appropriate. One way to guide children while allowing independence is to offer two viable options: "Do you want to clean up your room Saturday or Sunday?" Allow your child to feel involved and empowered in decisions outside the limits you set.

That said, avoid negotiating when you really believe a limit is needed. It's easy to fall into a cycle of nagging or cajoling in an effort to convince your child he should know better. For example, maybe you want to limit his screen time, so you try to convince him that excessive screen time isn't healthy and he should go play in the yard. If you intend to limit screen time, limit screen time. If you want to collaboratively discuss it, that's great, but it isn't a limit.

Create a Token Economy

For older children, a behavioral tool called a token economy can be used to tie together rewards (discussed in chapter 6) and limits. Eventually, although sometimes not until adolescence, children begin to connect their current actions with their long-term experience.

Start by letting your child earn larger rewards over greater amounts of time as part of an ongoing effort to emphasize positive actions. Then, to create a token economy, add limits to the mix by also taking away points for misbehavior. This takes patience, as children, even teens, can become unmotivated if they lose more than win. Define methodical small steps forward that allow for incremental success.

Utilize Lost Privileges

Every once in a while, a major behavioral issue may arise that falls outside your plan. You can then take away one of your child's privileges as punishment. Examples include losing access to a smartphone or being grounded for a weekend. Whenever possible, decide ahead of time on the details of what your child will lose and for how long. That way you'll have a plan in place if you need it.

With unanticipated situations, you'll need to devise a strategy in the moment. The first step is to pause. Tell your child that there will be a larger consequence, then calmly consider your choices only after you've taken a moment to settle yourself.

If there's a constant cycle of lost privileges and epic meltdowns, return to the basics earlier in this chapter and in chapter 6. Also reevaluate from the perspective of executive function, considering what strategies you might use to directly compensate for your child's ADHD. If an ongoing pattern persists, consider seeking help from a professional.

Q&A

Q: What if I set a limit and then realize I was wrong?

A: Whatever limits you may try to uphold, you'll screw up at times. You may blame your child for being late, only to realize you told him the wrong time. When you make mistakes, it's okay to admit that you're at fault and make amends. After all, being honest (and non-judgmental) is important too.

Setting Limits for Behavior Outside the Home

When you're at home or alone with your family, enforcing limits tends to be more straightforward. In the public eye, the stakes feel higher, and you may feel constrained about acting decisively.

To the extent possible, anticipate challenges that may arise in public settings and come up with specific behavioral plans for each. Follow the same basic framework of targeted praise, rewards, and setting and enforcing clear limits. Then explain your expectations to your child before going out. Start with an emphasis on appropriate behaviors: "If you collect ten points for conducting yourself well at the restaurant, you'll earn a Lego box." You can even have your child earn rewards during the situation itself: "If you behave for the first half of the flight, you can watch a movie of your choice during the second half."

During lengthy outings, offer distractions such as games, books, puzzles, or gift-wrapped toys. Also schedule breaks if you can. For example, hold a movie in reserve until you sense the tension rising but before problem behavior occurs. Or if you have two flights, let your child run around somewhere appropriate during the layover. Plan for these diversions well in advance.

Here's a checklist that can help you navigate difficult situations outside the home.

- [ ] **Anticipate.** What are the most difficult situations outside your home? Focus on coming up with plans for these ahead of time.

☐ **Modify the environment and your expectations.** Revisit the model of ADHD as a delay in executive function. If your child were five years younger, what would you expect of him? How would you try to modify the situation?

☐ **Set expectations for your child.** Discuss ahead of time how you expect your child to behave.

☐ **Use rewards.** Establish clear rewards for good behavior and help your child remember the potential reward.

☐ **Use limits.** Be clear about what you won't tolerate and the consequences for exceeding that limit. Time-outs are possible even outside the home, depending on the setting.

☐ **Picture how you'll act and what you'll say.** What would be the most skillful way for you to act in the moment? Take some time to envision your tone of voice, posture, body language, and so on.

Of course, unanticipated challenges will sometimes arise. In these situations, bear in mind this medical saying: "During an emergency, check your own pulse first." Steady yourself as best you can before dealing with the situation. You can't engage in flexible, creative problem solving if you're swamped by stress and fearful of what might happen. Be honest, take responsibility, and then remove your child from the situation if possible. Utilize a time-out if it seems needed and the situation allows for it.

Also monitor your inner critic. It may have a lot more to say about the situation than anyone observing you. Give yourself credit for trying and recognize how hard it is to manage whatever is going on. The moment will pass, and you and your child will both almost certainly get a chance to handle things more smoothly in the future.

Practice: Grounding Yourself

Upholding limits can be hard. If your child is swinging from the chandelier at a family event, you may feel like everyone's attention is focused on his misbehavior and your response. How can you remain reasonably balanced while effectively managing the situation and keeping your own embarrassment in check? Here's an informal mindfulness practice you can try.

In a difficult moment, start with a brief STOP or Fifteen Breaths practice. This creates an opportunity to bring your attention where you choose instead of getting caught up in an internal mental swarm.

Physical sensations in particular can provide a focus other than swirling thoughts and emotions. If you're standing, feel the pressure of your feet on the floor. If you're sitting, feel the surface you're sitting upon. Anchor yourself to this physical base, and, as best you can, attend to that one, less highly charged aspect of your experience.

For a few moments, set aside trying to fix anything. Meanwhile, continue to monitor your experience as in the practice Watching the Weather, in chapter 4. As you gather your resources, reconnect with your intentions before deciding what to do next.

Common Obstacles with Limits

In spite of knowing better, we don't always uphold established limits with our children. It's common to fall back on old habits when we're off balance. This can happen in any area of life, which is why mindfulness traditions offer guidance for overcoming some of the most common habitual behaviors and attitudes that can be obstacles to acting on our intentions.

Having habits isn't inherently wrong. We may settle into household routines that keep the day moving, or develop unconscious ways to calm our children. But sometimes habits are less useful, like eating when bored, yelling when angry, or blaming others when we feel guilty.

Simply paying attention to habits, without judgment or expecting perfection, is an important aspect of developing new options. Even for habits that are difficult to change, awareness allows for more active decision making. Here are some common mental habits that may undermine behavioral planning.

Grasping

In the context of mindfulness, "grasping" means holding on to a picture of how things "should" be. We instinctually hold on to what we like, including ideals of how our kids should act. But setting limits depends on having an objective view of your child's development—one that may not fit your ideal.

Grasping can create a desperate desire to control things, trying to make life fit our vision of the way things ought to be. You might avoid giving rewards or setting limits due to a belief that they shouldn't be needed because your child should know better. You can exhaust yourself in efforts to make everything fit your expectations.

Grasping also heightens many challenging situations, including getting caught up in how your child should behave. Maybe it seems as though a three-year-old should understand why he shouldn't hit other kids, but yours doesn't, or hits other kids anyway. If you hold on to these kinds of "shoulds," you may not see the fundamental need for new interventions, different activities, or clearer discipline.

Grasping can also undermine easy moments due to fear that they'll pass too soon. For one perfect moment, your child angelically curls up against your side. And you think, *This is great. If only I was this calm all the time, he'd be so much happier. It's probably my fault. No, it's really him. If he wasn't easily upset, we could do this all the time. I'm sure he's going to flip out any minute now.* And then the moment passes, its simple perfection lost amidst internal chatter.

Aversion

We avoid what we don't like and push away from things that seem unpleasant. That's natural. Perhaps you have a picture of ideal parenting in which children rarely cry, arising either from your own sense of compassion or because a parenting book suggested this is actually possible. So when your kid melts down because he wants that toy in aisle three, you capitulate. In a calmer moment, you might be able to hold firm, realizing that overindulgence isn't beneficial. But if you're fearful or upset, you're more likely to choose actions based on avoiding something stressful.

Maybe you struggle with enforcing limits or another aspect of parenting and can't figure out why, but avoid seeking help out of worry that you'll be judged for not being, able to do it on your own. Or maybe you judge yourself for the seeming weakness underlying your difficulty. Aversion is natural, but it can undermine decision making and behavior management. Accepting things as they are, even when they're unpleasant, allows for more success in setting and enforcing limits.

Feeling Overwhelmed or Burned-Out

Sometimes parenting a child with ADHD, or life in general, may feel like too much to manage. You may have a metaphorical—or literal—urge to go back to bed and pull the covers over your head. You may experience a mental fog or lack of energy that prevents you from handling a situation as best you can.

At any particular moment, it may feel easier to let your kid do whatever he wants: going to bed late, making questionable food choices, having poor manners, skipping chores… It can feel easier to just let it go. Maybe you're also dealing with sleep problems, perhaps because your child wakes you up for nights on end. When you're rundown, it's all too easy to let things slide, despite your intentions otherwise.

Restlessness

Sometimes you may feel impatient and want to force changes to happen right away. You might impulsively toss out your entire behavioral plan, even though in a better moment you'd accept that some short-term discomfort may be unavoidable when following a long-term plan to ease the situation. When anger, anxiety, or uncertainty arises, it can take over, causing you to leap into action rather than sticking with a well-considered strategy.

Self-Doubt

And then there is parenting doubt, in drips or deluges, arising and receding like the tides: *I should know better, I don't have the strength to change this, If only I were more like my sister*, and on and on. Once again, the inner critic nags, heckles, or worse. By noticing and labeling it, you can more easily let it go. The self-compassion exercise in chapter 6, Give Yourself a Real Break, may also be helpful.

Exercise: Bringing Mindfulness to Setting Limits

Over the next several days, notice your personal style around limits. Maybe you're too lenient or inconsistent in your message. Maybe you're too strict. Maybe you're battling a sense of fatigue that limits your ability to be consistent. When difficult moments around limits arise, notice the thoughts, emotions, and physical sensations that arise for you. Also notice any tendencies toward grasping, aversion, feeling overwhelmed, restlessness, or self-doubt.

In each instance where limits aren't working well, bring both compassion and awareness to investigating why. Maybe new limits are called for as your child grows up. Maybe you made a choice that hasn't worked out and you need to adjust it. Or maybe, when you pause to reflect, you'll see that in spite of your worries, everything is working well.

What is your intention, and what do you actually do? Label this habit, then reflect on what you'd like to do instead. If this involves trying something new, write down the situation and the new response you'd like to use. Here are some examples:

- *When I feel myself getting overwhelmed, I'll walk away and practice mindfulness for a few minutes.*

- *When I feel the urge to make a barbed comment to my child, I'll refrain and stay silent.*

- *When I'm about to give in to a tantrum, I'll stick to the plan and send my child to time-out instead.*

Habits are hard to change. Expect that you'll fall back into old patterns many times. Pause often and take a deep breath. When you manage a situation as you intended to, even if it happens only once a day or once a week, pay attention to that and give yourself full credit for the accomplishment.

The Two Wings of Mindfulness

A classic metaphor about mindfulness is that compassion and paying attention objectively (seeing the world clearly as it is) are the two wings of a bird. Each is required in equal measure to find wisdom. And so it is with parenting, which requires a similar balance. We aim for endlessly empathetic parenting paired with a realistic sense of our own strengths and limitations, our children's, and our role in guiding our children through life.

Action Plan: Addressing Challenging Behaviors

Sitting in meditation, we build skills. During those few minutes, we're electing not to act on what arises. We practice observing thoughts, emotions, and sensations with less reactivity. By creating a gap between what we encounter and what we do about it, we open the door to new approaches to old situations. All of these benefits are enormously helpful in navigating the challenges of setting and enforcing limits. So as you set about the following tasks, bring both wings of mindfulness, compassion and objectivity, to bear on behavioral planning for your child.

☐ Remain committed to your mindfulness practice. It will help you weather the storms that come with setting and enforcing limits. Set a daily practice time and write it here:

_____

☐ Decide which behaviors are currently most disruptive and write them here:

_____

_____

_____

_____

☐ Can any of these behaviors be addressed by externalizing the system and providing developmentally appropriate guidance to your child? If so, write the specifics of how you'll do so here:

_____

_____

_____

☐ Are there any behavioral triggers that can reasonably be avoided? If so, write them here:

_____

_____

_____

☐ Are there any behaviors that you might ignore for now, and that may diminish on their own if they don't succeed in grabbing your attention? If so, write them here:

_____

_____

_____

☐ Are there any behaviors for which it would be safe and reasonable to allow your child to experience the natural consequences? If so, write them here:

_____

_____

_____

☐ Choose up to three behaviors around which you intend to set limits and implement time-outs:

_____

_____

_____

Chapter 8

ADHD Goes To School

Read this chapter to...

- Understand the far-ranging effects of ADHD and executive function issues on learning

- Institute an effective educational plan for your child

- Help manage your child's homework and use it to teach organizational skills

- Bring mindfulness to collaboration with schools and the task of navigating your child's academic challenges

Strong, effective educational planning begins with understanding the impacts of ADHD and executive function issues on learning. Many skillful, bright teachers, psychologists, and therapists may engage with your child. They may spend extensive time with her and bring considerable training and expertise to these interactions. They may also have ideas and insights that challenge or change your point of view.

Conversely, helping kids with ADHD isn't a mandatory part of teacher education, so your child's teachers may not have the same knowledge you do. Therefore, in sorting out academic decisions, you may face the additional task of educating educators and negotiating for your child's needs.

Staying calm yet resolute during discussions about your child's future isn't always easy; anxiety, anger, and other intense emotions may beset you. It's a high art to remain open to others' opinions while advocating for what you feel matters most. Skillful communication will make collaborative, productive solutions more likely.

This is the heart of mindfulness: building resilience and a capacity to handle uncertainty, and encouraging personal traits that increase well-being and enhance interactions with the world. Through mindfulness, you can bring flexibility and responsiveness to figuring out what to do when your child has misbehaved at school or failed a class. In these ways, a practice of mindfulness can support you in collaborating with others to create an effective educational plan for your child.

Steady as You Go

Responsiveness depends on being able to notice when you're riled up and then finding a bit of space to decide what to do instead of reacting thoughtlessly. Whenever you notice yourself surging toward reactivity, take a mindful breath or two. For most of us, life provides lots of opportunity for practice.

The essence of mindfulness is to find a middle path that allows you to experience life with ease and joy. When you feel too intent and wrapped up in the turmoil of the moment, come back to your practice and let go of striving for a few moments. When your approach seems too lax or avoidant, take a few moments to set a renewed intention for moving forward.

The art of paying attention doesn't entail a draconian demand for vigilant focus; it's more akin to picking up a delicate glass. Some effort is required; otherwise, you'll let the glass slide from your fingers. But with too strong a grip the glass shatters, and with too much intensity you may knock it over. Somewhere in between, you safely lift the glass and take a drink.

How Executive Function Affects Classroom Performance

School places high demands on children's executive function and requires a great deal of self-management. Beyond issues with focus or behavior, executive function is required for learning itself, which calls on the ability to manage attention, actions, tasks, information, emotions, and effort. For children with ADHD, individualized academic planning that takes these capacities into account is necessary for maintaining motivation and supporting success.

Even a very basic task, such as writing down daily assignments, can require numerous executive function–based steps:

- Paying attention when the assignment is given (attention management)

- Having a strategy for remembering details, such as a day planner (task management)

- Prioritizing writing the assignment over any other activity (action management and task management)

- Remembering the location of the day planner (information management)

- Finding the planner in time to use it (attention management and effort management)

- Tracking down a pencil (attention management, information management, and task management)

- Holding the information in mind long enough to get it on paper (information management) without procrastinating or assuming it can be written down later (task management)

- Writing it legibly (action management)

- Moving the planner back to an established place (task management)

Academic success doesn't depend on effort alone. Executive function underlies everything from activities as simple as getting out the door in the morning to complex undertakings like coordinating a long-term project. We can only teach children what they need to know after we've accurately identified any struggles related to ADHD and executive function.

No "Should" in Schooling—Only Can or Cannot

There's a common misperception that children with ADHD *should* be able to accomplish their schoolwork solely through their own effort and sense of responsibility. But the fact is, a fifteen-year-old who has the executive function skills of a ten-year-old requires the support you'd give a ten-year-old, despite facing high school level academic demands. You can "should" your child, yourself, and her school all you want, but either she can or cannot do it.

"Should" statements often create distress for parents, teachers, and students. If "should" means "how most peers handle the situation," then that desired behavior may provide a useful reference point in advocating for why your child needs academic services. But if you feel your child should manage homework better because of her age, that doesn't resolve the situation. Her skills are what they are right now and can't be anything else.

In fact, you probably don't mean "should" in a literal sense. You mean, "Other kids her age do," or "I expected that by the time she was fourteen I wouldn't be involved in her homework." This comparison to what should be happening probably adds to the stress of dealing with your child's ADHD.

In any situation, there are facts, and then there are all the thoughts and emotional responses we add to them. Notice the difference between thoughts that carry you toward a solution and those that add to your troubles. Without suppressing anything, continue to refine a sense that you don't need to take all thoughts at face value. Then, as the nuances become clearer, choose what you can do next to best support your child.

When Is ADHD Underdiagnosed?

The children most often missed by ADHD rating scales are those who are primarily inattentive. They may be well-behaved and have academic skills that allow them to keep up, even though they aren't thriving.

Girls especially (but not exclusively) may sit quietly in a classroom but wrestle internally with disorganization, self-management, and daydreaming. Such kids may struggle with stress, anxiety, or social concerns. They usually work many times harder than their peers to achieve similar results, diminishing their self-esteem and causing them to feel overwhelmed.

Educational law protects all children with ADHD regardless of their test scores and grades. Identifying children with this inattentive type of ADHD allows parents and teachers alike to provide the structure and guidance necessary for them to develop both confidence and the academic skills that will help them excel.

Executive Function and Educational Policy

From classroom design to curriculum, modern schools tend to place huge demands on children's executive function. These extreme expectations often start in kindergarten, with academic tasks far beyond the developmental ability of many five-year-olds. Fourth-grade classrooms seemingly require what used to be a sixth-grade level of self-regulation and planning, a dynamic that persists through high school. For a child with ADHD, already years behind in executive function skills, there's an increasing gap between what's expected and their actual skills.

Smaller, well-structured classrooms that minimize distraction go a long way in helping all students learn, especially those with ADHD. Yet in recent decades, classes have gotten larger, often with dozens of students and just one adult. Layout is frequently in desk clusters, with children sitting in a circle. Yet research indicates that it's easier for students to pay attention when they directly face the teacher (Hastings and Schwieso 1995). Desk clusters promote distractibility and off-task behaviors; this is why auditorium seats face forward.

Traditional approaches have relied on sustained instruction for the basic building blocks in any subject. This makes sense. If you ask experts in almost any field, they'll tell you that automatic fluency in the basics is a necessary prerequisite to acquiring advanced skills. You can't play a Mozart sonata without first learning to play scales. As stated in the journal *American Educator*, "While experts often thrive without much guidance, nearly everyone else thrives when provided with full, explicit instructional guidance (and should not be asked to discover any essential content or skills)… Decades of research clearly demonstrate that *for novices* (comprising virtually all students), direct, explicit instruction is more effective and more efficient than partial guidance" (Clark, Kirschner, and Sweller 2012, 6; emphasis in original).

These traditional techniques are presently out of fashion in many mainstream public school settings. Popular programs rely on experiential learning and play down the crucial need for a solid academic base built through routine and memorization.

What does this type of less-effective learning look like? Silent reading is emphasized. For children with ADHD who are distractible, impulsive, and lagging in reading skills, this reflects an often unrealistic expectation that they'll focus, behave, and be productive during unsupervised reading time. In writing, children who struggle with organizing their thoughts are expected to create coherent essays without first drafting a linear outline. In math, children who are still not fluent in the basics are pushed not only to solve higher-level problems but to explain their work in detail, which again relies on getting organized ideas onto paper.

A vicious cycle develops. Demands on executive function go up anytime a person faces something unfamiliar. When schools don't emphasize teaching basic facts, on some level nearly everything remains unfamiliar for kids. And while they're already maxed out in terms of assimilating new information, the curriculum marches on and the academic gap grows.

In addition, many children with ADHD also have a learning disability. If every child with asthma had a 60 percent chance of having kidney disease too, would we screen for kidney disease? Probably so. However, once ADHD is diagnosed, further testing may not occur because of an assumption that ADHD explains everything. If a child with ADHD has severe or persistent academic problems despite accommodations for ADHD, full educational testing is in order.

Whatever the situation, you and your child's teachers can best support your child by not expecting her academic skills to develop spontaneously. Right now, today, she may not have the capacity to focus, control her impulses, or manage her homework or a host of other academic tasks. As at home, she may require an intensive short-term safety net that essentially fills the gaps in her executive function. Then, as her skills develop, you can hand responsibilities back to her in measured ways that promote motivation, independence, and academic success.

Getting to the Root of the Problem

If your child is struggling academically, you need to identify all potential causes:

- **Evaluate for ADHD.** If you haven't already, obtain a broad assessment that considers executive function difficulties. Most schools will not, by policy, diagnose ADHD. You'll need to seek out a qualified professional, as discussed in chapter 1.

- **Evaluate for learning disabilities.** If ADHD accommodations don't improve your child's academic performance, have psychoeducational testing done to determine whether learning disabilities are an issue. Parents have the right to ask the school to provide such testing, or it can be conducted by an outside specialist.

- **Evaluate for other conditions.** With school personnel or whomever else you consult, consider common conditions that co-occur with ADHD that may be affecting your child's academic performance, such as anxiety or delays in language or fine motor skills.

Understanding How You Can Influence the System

There are, of course, limits to what a parent can do to influence school systems, teachers, classrooms, and curricula. Still, there are many avenues by which you can intervene and advocate for your child. So let's take a look at educational approaches that may better support your child and how you can guide them.

Due to executive function challenges, children with ADHD face numerous academic challenges. Impulsivity and distractibility lead to mistakes as children read words inaccurately or skip them. Poor working memory compromises both comprehension of text and completion of multistep math problems. Poor planning and organization make writing and long-term assignments difficult. And since children with ADHD have trouble with sustained cognitive effort, they end up avoiding the practice necessary to become fluent in skills in the first place.

The selection of instructional programs for children with ADHD is critical. Students with ADHD are especially prone to academic difficulties when schools don't spend enough time making basic skills automatic. These students need direct instruction, repetition, and monitored practice, with teachers providing correction and feedback.

Beginning reading programs should have a heavy emphasis on phonics and oral reading under adult supervision. For children who also have a reading disability, an appropriate program should integrate spelling and handwriting in what's called an Orton-Gillingham or multisensory approach. Eventually, students need to be taught how to underline, annotate, and take notes as they read.

A strong math program will provide sufficient enough practice in number facts that children commit them to memory. Learning simple, step-by-step solutions to basic operations, such as subtraction with borrowing and double-digit multiplication, is vital. Finally, an effective writing program should incorporate strategies for outlining, editing, and revising compositions. Research papers and long-term projects should be used as vehicles for teaching how to break down projects into logical steps and manage them over time.

As for what you can do, start by educating yourself about ADHD in academic environments. Familiarize yourself with the broad range of supports children with ADHD are entitled to by law. Encourage your child's school to implement a wide-ranging plan that provides what your child needs to thrive and develop strong academic motivation. If you feel a school isn't meeting your child's needs, consult with an outside specialist, such as a physician, psychologist, or educational advocate familiar with this field.

While you probably can't influence a school's decisions about instructional programs, you can still request the kind of curricula described above. If such approaches aren't offered in the school's mainstream classes, they might be in special education. If you feel that your child's school isn't teaching effectively, try to find the necessary instruction in another venue, such as a different classroom, with a tutor, or, as a last resort, at a new school. You also can try teaching basic skills to your child at home if you can work together without creating additional stress.

Q&A

Q: What can I do about my child's handwriting? She can't even read her own notes.

A: Many children with ADHD have difficulty with handwriting, a problem exacerbated by the fact that many schools no longer emphasize handwriting instruction. The ability to write quickly and legibly relies on learning to write before bad habits develop. That means utilizing direct instruction and having children practice printing, typically through second grade, and learning cursive starting in third grade. Once those windows of opportunity have been missed, keyboarding may be the only option, and then only along with an effective program with sufficient typing practice. It's still worth developing handwriting skills when possible, because handwritten notes tend to reinforce learning better. If need be, ask for writing instruction as part of your child's educational plan or seek a tutor.

Creating an Academic Plan

Educational law in the United States lays out two potential avenues for children with ADHD in public schools: Section 504 plans and Individualized Education Programs (IEPs). Private schools aren't bound by these laws but may choose to follow the recommendations anyway.

- **Section 504 accommodations** protect a child's integration into mainstream classrooms. This law covers any physical disability at school, including ADHD. Grades don't determine whether a child qualifies for Section 504 accommodations. A child who's getting good marks but struggling due to ADHD still qualifies. This is one reason why having a diagnosis of ADHD can be helpful for your child.

- **Individualized Educational Programs** are broader special education interventions that include services outside the mainstream, from separate classrooms to different forms of therapy (speech-language, occupational, or physical therapy) to academic interventions for which a child is pulled out of the classroom. Because IEPs tend to be more major interventions, schools often consider an IEP before moving on to discussion of a 504 plan. Once implemented, an IEP typically covers details specific to ADHD, so a 504 plan isn't needed.

When meeting with educators about the academic choices available for your child, remember mindfulness. Pause if you become concerned about the direction of conversation. If you're confused, ask for clarification. If you feel a recommendation is inappropriate, know that you have the right to disagree. Take notes and, afterward, consider everything that was said. If you work with a therapist or other professional on your child's ADHD, consult that person before agreeing to any plan.

During school meetings, use the following checklist (download available) to inquire about accommodations that may be available for your child. Seek out both short-term solutions that adapt to your child's present skills and a long-term plan for independence. Include instruction for your child in both academic and organizational skills, or consider hiring a psychologist, coach, or tutor to help your child in these areas. Identify who will coordinate your child's plan at school, both as a resource for your child and as your own link for communication; often this will be a teacher, school psychologist, social worker, or guidance counselor.

Classroom accommodations

- ☐ Preferential seating in the front of room, facing the teacher, and away from children who are particularly distracting

- ☐ Minimization of distractions through a well-organized classroom, possibly with partitioned areas for independent work

- ☐ Scheduled breaks and shorter periods of sustained effort

- ☐ Prompting for transitions between activities

- ☐ Written routines or visual schedules for nonreaders and adherence to those routines

- ☐ Frequent parent-teacher communication about schoolwork, along with an early warning system. (If homework is missed or anything changes academically, it's easier to problem solve early.)

Homework and organizational accommodations

☐ Prompting your child to write down assignments, and not relying on online systems unless all teachers in the school are committed to using them daily

☐ Plans for redirecting your child when off task

☐ A daily organizational check-in for your child with a teacher or other staff member

☐ Breaking up projects into daily portions and helping your child record the steps on a calendar, along with adult monitoring of progress for each step

☐ Daily logistical support, such as how to get to classes without being late, managing books, and organizing a locker

☐ Reminders to hand in homework and projects (or allowing them to be scanned and e-mailed directly to teachers)

☐ Offering writing supports, such as outlines, and making them available whenever needed

☐ Handwriting supports, such as allowing keyboarding, along with additional writing instruction

☐ Supplying written notes for each class

☐ Providing duplicate textbooks so one copy can be kept at home and the other at school

☐ Modifying homework to ensure a reasonable workload per evening

Behavioral planning

☐ Using reward-based behavioral plans, with positive feedback outweighing negative, and rewarding productive behaviors, such as self-checking schoolwork

☐ Frequent communication with you regarding your child's behavior

☐ Consistent routines in the classroom

☐ Not utilizing punishments that involve loss of gym and recess time, since exercise often diminishes ADHD symptoms and kids with ADHD need more breaks during the day

Testing modifications

☐ Extending test time as needed. (Some children with ADHD rush regardless; extended time only helps those who work slowly.)

☐ Testing away from distractions

☐ Reading test instructions to your child

☐ Providing writing supports

☐ Checking for careless errors

☐ Using alternate testing methods as needed (for example, oral versus written)

Making the Most of Homework

When homework dominates life, it no longer has any benefit. As mentioned, the national recommendation is around ten minutes per grade, maximum. Any more cuts into vital activities like sleep, downtime, family time, and hobbies. It's also exhausting. Excess homework often undermines motivation and increases academic stress, especially for kids with ADHD.

Children with strong executive function skills may intuitively keep a to-do list and manage their time, strategies that are entirely foreign to those with ADHD. For them, making homework manageable requires an effective plan that externalizes the system by establishing a homework time, a routine, and adult supervision.

Homework expectations rise as children get older, so you'll probably need to step back in to help periodically. A child who's developed the ability to manage in seventh grade may begin to struggle in high school or even college. Anticipate this and monitor your child's performance, particularly at the start of the school year, even if she has been doing well.

Creating a Basic Homework Plan

Establishing a routine will make homework go more smoothly and build skills for a lifetime. Here's how to go about it.

Create a Homework Space with Minimal Distraction

Find a work space away from toys, screens, and anything else overly distracting. If your child requires adult supervision, set up a work space that's easily accessible but not in the midst of household distractions (like at the kitchen table during meal preparation).

Schedule a Homework Start Time

By nature, children with ADHD procrastinate, prioritize poorly, and get overly focused on play. Scheduling a consistent routine will help your child learn to do the most important tasks first. Consider building in a break of about fifteen minutes for a snack or running around, avoiding video games or other activities that are hard to stop. Encourage playdates and after-school activities, and then create a consistent plan for those days too.

Allow for Timed Breaks

Children often focus more easily when they know a break awaits. Use a timer, choosing an amount of work time comfortable for your child—anywhere from fifteen to forty-five minutes, depending on age. Allow five- to ten-minute breaks, and time both work and breaks—otherwise the breaks may drag on. During breaks, avoid activities that are hard to transition away from.

If your child is in middle school or high school, consider asking her to estimate how long she thinks each segment of homework might take, then compare those guesses with what actually happens: "You thought you'd get your math done in half an hour, but it took an hour." This will help her recognize any tendency to overestimate or underestimate.

Create a Homework To-Do List

Utilize a daily checklist with specific steps. It might look something like this, depending on your child's age:

- Confirm that you have a list of your homework assignments.

- ☐ Confirm that you have all the materials you need.

- ☐ Complete your homework, checking off each item on your assignment list as soon as you're done.

☐ After completing each assignment, check your work for mistakes.

☐ Put your homework in your backpack in its appropriate place.

☐ Put your backpack where it belongs.

As for that backpack, which may be a disorganized disaster, having a brightly colored, separate folder for things that need to be handed in can help with forgetfulness. Encourage your child to develop a habit of putting each piece of homework in that folder immediately upon completing it. Encourage her (or a teacher) to check the folder at school. If it's empty by the end of the day, this confirms that everything has been handed in.

Provide Supervision

Your only job in regard to your child's homework should be to make sure your child is on task and answer general questions. If you have to be more involved, reconsider the overall routine, whether further accommodations for her ADHD are needed, or whether the homework needs to be modified in some way.

Make Sure Your Child Understands the Homework

The function of homework is to reinforce what's learned in school. If your child consistently doesn't understand assignments or takes too long because the work is too difficult, ask her teachers to adjust the content. If your child needs to learn new concepts to complete the homework, it's too hard. It's okay to leave it partially completed and send it back with a note to her teacher.

Consider Offering Rewards for Completing the Homework Routine

Earning points toward rewards can motivate your child to complete her homework routine. If you go this route, consider making maintaining a good attitude a condition for earning the points.

Monitor for ADHD Symptoms

If your child can't concentrate because of ADHD, she simply can't concentrate. She may still benefit from everything outlined above, but if ADHD is preventing her from progressing, it may be time to reevaluate her larger treatment plan.

Teaching Organizational Skills Through Homework

As you begin to manage your child's ADHD, early on you may be constantly putting out fires. Later you can act more like a coach, taking someone who's already doing well to the next level. And though it may be a struggle at first, you can use homework to teach your child skills vital for self-managing her ADHD.

ADHD involves deficits in planning that undermine efficiency, so your child may come up with homework systems that waste time and energy or aren't adaptable as demands rise. She may reach the point where she gets good grades and manages to hold everything together, yet a ramshackle organizational system or poor study skills still add unnecessary time demands or stress. So once you've moved beyond any acute academic problems, use homework as an opportunity to cultivate good skills in writing, studying, time management, and other tasks related to executive function.

Emphasize Using a To-Do List

Mentally keeping track of everything takes energy and makes forgetting details more likely. And with ADHD, even memorized routines can dissolve under pressure. Establishing a to-do list for homework will teach your child to rely on concrete, written lists to reduce the strain and minimize mistakes.

Use a Calendar to Teach Planning and Time Management

Choose a weekly time, perhaps Sunday night, to review the upcoming week. If your child seems old enough, help her set up a calendar for herself. Include both homework and other after-school activities so she can adequately plan the week ahead. Help her break long-term school assignments into smaller, scheduled work sessions. Guide her in developing foresight and planning by pointing out conflicts ahead of time: "You'll need to work on your project Wednesday because Thursday night you have practice for the play." If your child is too young for this, keep a family schedule and use it to help her build a concept of time, pointing out when fun things are on the horizon, which days will be busy, any birthdays or holidays, and so on.

Gradually Transition to Independence

By following a few basic steps, you can help your child become independent in any skill related to organization. Homework is a great place to start. Just be aware that months of reinforcement may be required before your child can take over on her own. This kind of transition is a three-stage process:

Stage 1: Complete the task with your child and then review it together.

Stage 2: Ask your child to complete the task while you supervise.

Stage 3: Once your child seems to have the skill down, step back and let her do it completely on her own while still monitoring her performance.

Clear the Decks of Homework Backlog

Students with academic challenges often manage well enough at the start of the school year but reach a common tipping point. Several months into the school year, they may experience an increase in demands, with more daily work, longer projects, or an added extracurricular activity, so they need to do a bit more each night than they can handle. The trickle of accumulating work eventually becomes a deluge. Between poor executive function, other ADHD difficulties, and stress, your child may implode academically.

The solution is a two-pronged approach. First, help your child clear the decks. Almost by definition, someone who's barely keeping up can't handle the required daily workload plus the extra effort required to catch up. See if you can negotiate a one-time amnesty from your child's teachers.

Second, revisit your child's homework plan and revise it as needed to provide more support around executive function challenges. Even a high school junior may have no concept of how to manage her time or keep a to-do list. Whatever your child's age, she'll need reminders from you and her teachers, along with daily monitoring, to help her sustain an externalized organization system.

High School Planning and ADHD

High schools usually approach academic support differently than in lower grades, assuming students can take responsibility for getting their work done. The expectation is that these kids should be able to manage their schedule, handle intense homework loads, hand everything in on time, and coordinate around after-school activities too.

For someone with ADHD, this may be too much to ask. Teenagers with ADHD may look and (mostly) act like their peers but have the executive function and self-monitoring skills of a ten-year-old. Expecting them to handle so much planning and communication is a setup for failure.

One common flaw is open-ended planning, where academic supports are available but unscheduled and voluntary. Getting to an after-school session requires many executive function skills: remembering to go, keeping track of time, putting aside fun activities, and maintaining the attention required to get to the session. This kind of planning also relies on the student to recognize that she needs help, then make a plan for getting help and sticking with it. For a child with ADHD, none of this is a given. The simplest way around any planning deficit is to schedule the service instead.

It might not seem to make sense that high school teachers would have to communicate with parents about schoolwork. Yet for particular students, that may be vital until they develop their own capacity to manage. Ideally, parents are kept in the loop and made aware within days if their child is falling behind.

As always, the bottom line is having a compassionate and objective view of your child's current skills. Seek a clear understanding of her capacity to manage, rather than leaving her to flail when she falls behind. Of course, many teens with ADHD don't want to be bothered with school planning. No matter how many explanations they've heard, they may not recognize how their ADHD interferes with life due to poor time management and procrastination, or why working on skills to overcome these difficulties would simplify life. Yet you can't just impose a schedule on a teen in the same way you would with a younger child.

ADHD is a planning deficit, so even the most motivated teen will have a hard time creating and sustaining a strategy to overcome her ADHD. Whether your teen is motivated or resistant, here are some tips on helping her with school planning and helping her reach her academic potential:

- Continue using adult-created academic and homework schedules as long as possible. After your teen starts managing her own time, encourage ongoing discussion of scheduling and logistics. If possible, sustain a weekly planning session with a calendar.

- Utilize outside resources, such as a psychologist or ADHD coach. Many teens reach a point where they won't take advice from their parents. In that case, negotiate an alternative: "If you commit to work with Dr. So-and-So, your father and I will leave you alone about school." Everyone wins. You can focus more on what's going well, and your teen will gain some of the independence she craves.

- Encourage self-monitoring. Challenge your teen to compare the effects of different approaches, such as two weeks of following a particular plan (like completing homework while her medication is still working) to two weeks without one. She's likely to find that, in the absence of a plan, work takes much longer, so she's wasting her own time.

- Use a token economy, as discussed in chapter 7. Encourage routines through a structured reward system, offering points for sticking to the plan—and keeping a good attitude while doing so. Define the basic framework you think necessary, then collaborate on the details, especially rewards.

Return to Mindfulness

Mindfulness builds skills that allow you to remain settled in the midst of life's storms. Like a raft on the ocean, you ride the swells buffeted by wind but stay afloat. The chaos swirls, and you hold steady by guiding attention back to the sensations of breathing or your feet on the floor. You can't wish the weather away, but you can ride it out with as much skill and grace as possible.

As an example, imagine you're at work and your phone rings. You see that, once again, it's the school psychologist. You're immediately angry, although you're not yet sure at whom. You ignore the call and become increasingly stressed about having to eventually return it.

Almost as if by magic, the school psychologist has reached across town and activated your fight-or-flight response, without you even picking up the phone. She may be sipping coffee during a break while reading a good book, but you want to toss your phone out the window. You don't even know for sure that anything has gone wrong; maybe your child did something spectacularly well.

What does meditation have to do with this? So often in life, what throws us off balance doesn't have anything to do with our immediate reality. We're in one place, and our minds are elsewhere. People are saying one thing—or saying nothing—and we're making assumptions about their attitude or intentions. And when there actually is something unpleasant, the mind complicates that moment too, adding layers of habitual judgments and fears.

Anytime you feel yourself getting riled up, consider a quick check-in, turning your attention to what you're bringing to the situation. Here's the process, using that call from the school psychologist as an example:

- **What's happening in your mind?** Perhaps you're thinking of previous calls from the school. There's nothing wrong with considering the past. In fact, by doing so, you might learn something. But maybe you're annoyed because you have other things to do, adding to your stress, or you're frustrated with yourself because you didn't get around to calling the school psychologist yourself, weeks ago. Perhaps you wish your spouse would field this one. Maybe you're frightened that your child has hit someone, has failed another test, or is getting thrown out of fifth grade, all of which are only guesses as to what might be happening.

- **What are you feeling emotionally?** You may be overwhelmed by a cascade of anger, fear, and anxiety. Each leads to more thoughts, sensations, and emotions, potentially leaving you flustered and unable to do the things that would help you get out of this stressful situation.

- **What's happening in your body?** Are you experiencing physical responses to stress, fear, and the fight-or-flight reaction, such as a racing heart, clenched fists, or feeling flushed and overheated? These kinds of sensations can lead to more tension, fear, anger, and anxious thoughts, again pushing you away from any peace you might find.

With mindfulness you can practice noticing and letting go or noticing and not wrestling quite so much. You can recognize that the thought *This conversation is going to bring me misery* is just a thought, not reality. Then you can choose to give yourself a break and skillfully decide upon a reasonable next step.

Your swirling inner experience can create pressure to explode outward into action or collapse inward on yourself. By focusing on what's actually going on for you, you can let the mental storm pass without investing in it—a good thing, as the effort of trying to force thoughts into submission or to just stop thinking only escalates them. Notice what happens when you create a little distance from your thoughts, observe them, and ride them out for a while.

There will be times when your child needs you to stand strong, and times when being too rigid will hold her back. There are times to let things slide, and times when being too passive would undermine her progress. The ability to notice any of these stances and choose what genuinely fits the situation takes calmness, clarity, and the ability to notice and break habits that don't serve you or your child well.

While mindfulness is often discussed as a method of building specific skills for individuals, it's meant to impact how we interact with the world. Educational planning can be a stressful and sometimes contentious experience. You ease the process when remaining calm and empathetic, not only about how ADHD is impairing your child in the classroom, but also about the stress and challenges everyone involved in negotiations brings to the table—including yourself.

To return to the example above, there's nothing to do next except make the call back to the school psychologist. Gather yourself and come back to your intentions for skillful communication in advocating for your child. What does your child most need from this upcoming conversation?

Practice: Mindful Movement

Mindfulness doesn't require stillness. There are times in life when you just want or need to move, and even then, you can practice mindfulness. In fact, many people find mindful movement easier than sitting meditation. It may also be easier to work into your schedule. When you're walking and enjoying the spring weather, walk and enjoy the spring weather, guiding your attention back to the experience whenever it wanders. That's mindfulness.

Walking meditation can be practiced in different ways. If you're limited by space, move back and forth over a short distance while paying attention to the detailed physical sensations of movement. Pay attention to the pressure of each foot on the floor, the shift of your body weight, and whatever else you notice while walking. You can pace yourself however you like.

Another option is to practice walking meditation wherever you are. Whether you're out in nature or pushing your way through city streets, stay aware and attuned to your immediate experience. No one else needs to know that you're practicing mindfulness. Keep your eyes open and take it all in—both internal and external experience. After all, if you pay too much attention to your internal experience, you might wander into traffic or step in a hole.

Given that you're a busy parent, take advantage of walking anywhere to practice mindfulness. On autopilot, you might walk ten blocks or go for an entire hike without really tuning in to your experience and your surroundings. Instead, notice noises, smells, sights, the feel of the air, the sensations of walking, and your thoughts and emotions.

Even just walking from your car to your house you can notice your mind moving into the house already: *Ugh, need to discuss homework.* When thoughts pull at you, notice them and then return to your footsteps. If you're on your way to a challenging meeting with your child's teachers, use a long hallway for a walking meditation to settle yourself.

You can use the same approach with other physical activities. Whether you're jogging, doing yoga, taking the stairs, or working out at the gym, an opportunity awaits to cultivate mindfulness.

Action Plan: Helping Your Child Succeed Academically

In your role as parent, you make decisions at home that you feel are best, coordinating only within your family. Around your child's education, your influence may seem far less direct, yet it can still be profound. By supporting your objectivity, compassion, and communication skills, mindfulness increases your ability to engage in creative, effective educational planning when interacting with administrators, teachers, and everyone else involved.

- [ ] If your child has persistent academic difficulties, seek out comprehensive testing.

- [ ] Negotiate for academic accommodations at school.

- [ ] Create a homework routine and help your child stick to it. The routine should incorporate these basics:

  - [ ] Setting up a homework space with minimal distractions

  - [ ] Establishing a set time for doing homework (though this may vary from day to day depending on extracurricular activities)

  - [ ] Allowing for timed breaks

  - [ ] Helping your child make and adhere to a homework to-do list

  - [ ] Possibly offering rewards for completing the homework routine

  - [ ] Using a calendar or weekly planner to enhance time management

- [ ] Practice mindfulness every day.

  - [ ] Continue your formal practice, including walking meditation if you like.

  - [ ] Continue your informal practice, with a focus on bringing mindfulness to negotiations about your child's academic plan, whether on the phone, via e-mails, or in meetings.

Chapter 9

Navigating ADHD Medication Decisions

Read this chapter to...

- Make informed decisions for or against ADHD medication

- Manage your child's ADHD medications to maximize benefits and minimize side effects

- Use mindfulness to guide you through emotionally charged decision making related to your child's ADHD

One of the central concepts behind mindfulness is this: Don't believe something only because someone else says it's true. If you see no benefit to mindfulness practice, adjust what you're doing or put it aside for a while. Nothing you read or hear will change your life unless you apply effort and experience it for yourself.

The same can be said about ADHD: Don't believe people just because they say something's true. The medication options you'll read about in this chapter are based on extensive research; some of the results of that research may seem intuitive to you, and some less so. If you remain uncertain about what to believe, check your sources and educate yourself, and continue to methodically and purposefully take action to address your child's ADHD. Also, note that this chapter should be helpful to you no matter where you stand in regard to medications, as it addresses overall decision making around ADHD—a common source of stress for parents.

As you consider various ADHD treatments, people may try to sell you stuff or scare you with horror stories. The intense weight of what-ifs may clamp down on you as you consider the options. All of this adds layers of pain to an already overwhelming choice. Finding solid ground requires responsiveness, flexibility of thought, and an objective view of the situation.

Also be aware that medication alone can't address all aspects of ADHD. Two-thirds of children with ADHD have co-occurring issues such as anxiety, learning disabilities, or developmental delays (MTA Cooperative Group 1999). In addition, not all executive function issues respond directly to medication, so these challenges may require parent- and teacher-driven behavioral plans and direct instruction. Lastly, while nearly 80 percent of children respond to medications without experiencing significant side effects, nearly one in five don't and therefore require other interventions (Hinshaw and Scheffler 2014).

Whether you're considering ADHD medication for your child for the first time or reassessing earlier decisions about this, remember that various behavioral and educational supports are integral to managing ADHD. And in spite of textbook recommendations to use medication from the start, a more measured approach is typically possible. If interventions other than medication allow your child to progress adequately, stick with them and reassess regularly. Month by month and year by year, make sure your child is meeting his potential. If his progress lags, rethink all the possible interventions, including medication.

Mindfulness and Uncertainty

There's a natural tendency to avoid whatever seems scary. When you're faced with a choice between two options, one apparently lower in risk and the other higher, you may naturally turn away from perceived danger. However, doing so reactively can thwart good decision making. Out of this kind of near terror, parents may buy yet another random educational product, sign up for an untested intervention, or simply refuse to listen to others' insights about their child. Instead of seeking the most skillful option, they react and avoid.

Major decisions can be stressful because often there isn't a single clearly superior option. This uncertainty creates angst. You understandably want the relief a definitive answer would seem to offer, even though it's seldom possible to make absolute statements about child development.

Like a willow tree in a storm, the most nuanced path is generally to bend with the wind while holding firm to the ground—to exhibit both strength and flexibility. Yet for most of us, there's a tendency to rigidly stick to our position, constricting around what we believe and refusing to relent at all: *That's something I'd never, ever consider doing.*

Often, underlying anxiety is a complicating issue. People tend to assume that fixing some problem will make the anxiety go away (and it will sometimes). But ultimately, accepting uncertainty as inevitable leads to less anxiety. We can run ourselves ragged searching for an answer to a problem that's 100 percent reliable, but because such solutions seldom exist, we doubt our choices before we make them, while making them, and afterward.

Clarity comes not from obsessive research or relentless rehashing of possibilities; it comes from acknowledging things as they are: *This is what I know, this is what I don't know, and nothing more is possible right now.* Being aware of feeling confused, we can perhaps become less enmeshed. We can recognize that not being able to know the future causes stress.

Bringing Mindfulness to Decision Making

How can you begin working differently with choices, medical or otherwise, around ADHD? Pause before making them whenever possible. Explore the situation by noting body sensations, thoughts, and emotions such as fear, anxiety, anger, or resentment. Seek the knowable facts, acknowledge your own experience, and also recognize what cannot be known.

Here's an approach you may find useful for any decision that challenges you:

1. Pause. Take time for a mindfulness practice, settling yourself as best you can and gathering your inner resources. Note any body sensations, thoughts, and emotions, such as fear, anxiety, anger, or resentment. Also be sure to notice whether stress or other emotions have made your thinking less flexible. If so, take some time for self-care before continuing with this process.

2. Aim to maintain awareness throughout the process of decision making and also when observing what follows. As always with mindfulness, notice what's actually happening, along with any thoughts, emotions, and bodily sensations.

3. Seek out objective information. The Internet is not always or even often an accurate source, particularly in regard to child development. Better sources include research-based studies, medical professionals, and mental health professionals. As you gather information, list potential pros and cons of each possible solution, sticking with information that seems to be based on research and solid facts.

4. Notice whether your inner critic is speaking up and what it's saying. Maybe someone implied your child should take ADHD medication and you weren't ready to consider that. Maybe someone implied children should never take ADHD medication, and your child is. Parenting is hard enough without these kinds of unasked-for public opinions, which tend to ratchet up worry and self-judgment.

5. Notice any tendency to make predictions about the future, especially catastrophizing about worst-case outcomes. Remember, you can't know what will happen. You can only make reasoned choices based on the resources at hand.

6. Once you've made a choice, allow time for it to take hold and approach the process with compassion for both your child and yourself. When people feel uncertain, there's a tendency to fret and micromanage in ways that can undermine decisions they've made.

7. After giving a solution enough time to prove itself—or not—pause again and reevaluate. Remain open to reassessing and readjusting. More important than getting every decision exactly right is being honest with yourself and others afterward and making new decisions as needed.

8. If you remain uncertain and concerned, seek out expert advice. There's no better sign of self-confidence than knowing when to ask for help.

ADHD Medication Angst

While no decision about medication for children should be taken lightly, decisions around those for ADHD have become particularly loaded. Even the language around ADHD medications has become biased. We *treat* asthma and eczema, yet for ADHD we've been conditioned to say we're *medicating* children.

One of the hardest aspects of making decisions about ADHD medications is the huge amount of highly charged, frequently inaccurate information on this topic. People tend to generalize their individual experiences, and they may have strong reasons for doing so. Perhaps their child had a negative reaction to ADHD medication. That's understandably upsetting. Meanwhile, when medication works well for children, their parents may not feel compelled to share that outcome with the world. As mentioned above, seek out information based on objective information and research, and also consult with a health care professional you trust—or two, if that will help you feel more confident.

There's no point in being for or against ADHD medication. No one wants their child to have to take medication for any health condition. Ideally, and as appropriate, health care professionals should initially seek solutions that don't require prescriptions. As you forge ahead into this difficult territory, keep these basic points about ADHD in mind:

- ADHD is a medical disorder in which a particular part of the brain—one responsible for self-management—isn't functioning as well as it could.

- ADHD medication aims to support typical performance within this area of the brain.

- As with any prescription, ADHD medication has potential benefits and potential side effects.

- The fact that someone else can abuse or misuse ADHD medications doesn't have much bearing on whether medication is useful for a person who actually has ADHD.

Seeing beyond any fears you may have, societal assumptions, and the general stress of having a child with ADHD will help you make more well-informed decisions regarding medication. Then, whatever you choose, monitor the results and remain open to readjusting. You can always discontinue your child's ADHD medication if you don't like what you see. Alternatively, if you choose against it and your child continues to experience difficulties, you always have the option to try medication later. Managing your child's ADHD is a long-term process, allowing plenty of opportunities to refine your approach along the way.

Facts vs. Myths

To make a balanced decision, you'll need to weigh the pros and cons of medication against the pros and cons if your child doesn't take medication. Like any prescription medication, those for ADHD have both benefits and downsides, including side effects. When side effects occur, they should end when the medication is stopped. As you work toward separating facts from myths, here are some basic truths about ADHD medications to consider:

- ADHD medications aren't inherently dangerous or addictive. Most parents can find a medication that, when managed well, benefits their child without *any* significant side effects. And when used appropriately, these medications can be stopped and started without dependency. They're classified as controlled substances because of their potential for abuse, not because of a known risk to individuals using them correctly.

- They don't increase the risk of substance abuse. People with ADHD, children and adults alike, are at risk for substance abuse because they have ADHD (Harstad and Levy 2014). ADHD medications don't increase the risk of trying illegal substances. In fact, studies strongly suggest that treating ADHD with medications decreases the risk for substance abuse (Harstad and Levy 2014).

- They can't cause long-term side effects unless they're taken long term. The most commonly used ADHD medications don't accumulate in the body. Both their benefits and their side effects last only a few hours. If side effects occur and the medication is discontinued, children typically return to baseline within the day.

- They don't change users' personalities. They help children do better with self-monitoring and self-management, allowing them to live up to their potential without taking anything away from who they are. Brain function improves, giving kids a better chance to act on what they already know.

- They don't deprive children of their creativity. When people with ADHD thrive, their ability to complete creative projects should improve. People with ADHD frequently end up with dozens of half-completed endeavors and nothing finished.

Potential Benefits of Medication

The most frequently discussed research involving ADHD medication is the Multimodal Treatment of ADHD (MTA) study, conducted in 1999. It compared groups of children receiving behavioral therapy, medication, or both. A fourth group received a diagnosis and then returned to their general pediatrician for treatment advice.

These were the results: Intensive behavioral therapy that included classroom and parental supports helped with emotional and family concerns related to ADHD, but not much with symptoms such as impulsiveness or inattention. For these children, anxiety and parental satisfaction were particularly improved. The group that received only ADHD medication had far better outcomes in terms of ADHD symptoms. The combined treatment group showed gains similar to those for children solely taking medication (MTA Cooperative Group 1999), while seeming to require smaller doses of medication.

One controversy that arose in response to the MTA study is that research results didn't indicate any long-term benefits to medication. But this has more to do with the study's duration than any shortcoming in it. The study wasn't intended to track long-term results. After the research ended, people were free to change, stop, or start ADHD medication as well as nonmedical ADHD treatments. And without data regarding what anyone chose to do after the study, it cannot be determined why the benefits faded (Arnold et al. 2008).

In fact, one of the most profound lessons of the MTA study may be that the observed benefits of the medications probably arose from how they were meticulously adjusted while tracking benefits and side effects. The take-home message is that careful management of medication is important. Unfortunately, this isn't always the standard of care in the real world.

There is even a small but increasing body of research suggesting that medications could have long-term benefits for kids with ADHD. We're a long way from certainty, but it seems that early medication interventions may decrease the long-term effects of ADHD on well-being, as the following studies indicate:

- Students experience academic gain. For example, one study showed that the longer children stayed on medication, the closer their academic skills advanced toward the level of their peers (Scheffler et al. 2009). Another study documented improvements in math and reading with medication (Zentall, Tom-Wright, and Lee 2013). Allowing children to keep up academically during early education may have significant benefits regardless of longer-term decisions.

- ADHD symptoms may diminish while executive function improves. Studies of young adults with ADHD who were no longer using medication show that those treated with medications in childhood reported fewer impairments due to ADHD than those who never used them (Powers et al. 2008).

- Brain imaging studies have begun to show potential neurological benefits, perhaps because of neuroplasticity. While more research is needed, it is possible that ADHD medication paves the way for more typical brain development (Spencer et al. 2013; Czerniak et al. 2013).

Far more research is needed into extended use of ADHD medications. That said, between studies already conducted and decades of extended use by many children, no long-term negative consequences have yet been identified. Ultimately, the decision about whether or when to stop these medications depends entirely on whether they are providing continued benefits.

Types of ADHD Medication

The first medications usually prescribed for a child with ADHD are stimulants. You may be surprised to learn that these medications have been prescribed to children for nearly eighty years. They're called stimulants because they stimulate regions of the brain involved in executive function, not because they stimulate the entire body.

For practical purposes, all stimulant medications have the same potential side effects and benefits. Some are based on methylphenidate (Ritalin) and others on dextroamphetamine (Adderall), and it isn't possible to predict who will respond well to one or the other. Differences exist between how the formulations are administered and the length of their effect, and each child responds in an individual way.

Nonstimulant medications can also increase function of the frontal lobes. Commonly used nonstimulants include extended-release guanfacine (Intuniv) and clonidine (Kapvay), and atomoxetine (Strattera). They aren't usually tried first only because they typically don't work as well as stimulants. However, they tend to have fewer side effects. Functionally, they also differ from stimulants in that their benefits may not show up until a child has been taking them for a week or more.

Some children respond best to a combination of these two types of medication. Although it hasn't yet been widely studied, there even may be a slight additive benefit to using them together. In addition, when the two medications are taken together, sometimes they each can be prescribed in smaller doses to produce adequate benefits without side effects.

ADHD medications have been studied in children as young as three years of age. Therefore, if your child has a clear diagnosis and intense impairments and nonmedical interventions fail, medication may be an option even for preschoolers.

Q&A

Q: Are ADHD medications safe if my child also has another psychiatric condition along with ADHD?

A: The short answer is yes, it's usually safe to try them. Just be aware that they may make other psychiatric conditions either better or worse. For example, ADHD can exacerbate anxiety, so treatment may improve daily functioning in ways that help your child experience less anxiety. On the other hand, stimulant medication has the potential side effect of increased anxiety. As with all medications, careful observation, awareness of potential side effects, and close follow-up are important for a safe trial.

Avoiding Side Effects

During the initial trial and error of figuring out the best medication for a child, side effects aren't always avoidable. But if you watch for them, you can make changes as needed. It's natural to feel overwhelmed when reading about all possible side effects, but to achieve the best treatment outcome for your child, it's important to monitor for them. And remember, once you get through the initial trial and error, there should be no significant side effects remaining.

One potential physical side effect is difficulty falling asleep. For most children, the solution requires nothing more than switching to a shorter-acting medication.

Another common concern is daytime appetite loss, which is the one side effect hardest to avoid. But as long as your child's total calorie intake is sufficient, this daytime change won't harm him. If his appetite is blunted in the middle of the day, he's likely to make up for lost calories in the morning and evening without prompting.

Eating at least something during lunch will, of course, help him have energy through the afternoon.

If your child experiences prolonged weight loss, consult with his doctor. It may be necessary to change the medication or dose. But because it can take several months for your child's body to adapt to the medication, it's important to keep track of weight over longer stretches of time, rather than day to day.

Other side effects include headaches or stomachaches and, of course, a longer list of less-common problems, as listed on the insert. Because mild side effects sometimes improve over time, you might consider watching them for a short period before deciding to make changes. If they persist, talk with your child's doctor about adjusting the medication.

Large studies of children with ADHD have found that medications don't appear to affect long-term growth, despite popular claims to the contrary (Harstad et al. 2014). They're also thought to be safe for the heart (McCarthy et al. 2009), though children with cardiac risk factors should be screened.

One of the more complex issues is that stimulants can trigger onset of motor or vocal tics, though this is rare. Stimulants aren't believed to cause these tics, as children with ADHD are at risk for them regardless of medication use. Be aware that tics tend to run in bunches, over several days or weeks, so this side effect may persist for a while after medication is stopped.

For any medication that affects the brain, it's crucial to monitor overall mood, anxiety, obsessiveness, and mental health in general. ADHD medications carry warnings about depression and many other even more serious effects on mental health. Fortunately, these side effects aren't common. More often, children experience milder effects, such as irritability or anxiousness; such problems should resolve upon stopping that particular medication.

Successful treatment leaves children at their best more consistently. In spite of that, many people falsely suggest that ADHD medications turn children into "zombies." Some children do become withdrawn and flat, but this is only due to an ill-fitting medication, and it will last only a few hours for a single dose. A different medication may not have this effect.

Managing ADHD Medication

Finding the right ADHD medication fit for your child will be a process of trial and error. If you monitor your child closely and consult with the prescribing physician as needed, you should end up with a medication your child tolerates well that also leads to significant improvement in ADHD symptoms.

As mentioned earlier, most doctors start with one of the stimulants. They're effective, short acting, and seem to be quite safe. They also all have the same risks and benefits. They vary primarily in length of effect, and even that fluctuates from person to person. They aren't dosed based on weight; rather, the doctor will start with a small dose and incrementally increase it as needed.

The benefits of stimulants don't accrue over time, as the benefits of nonstimulants do. What you see right away is what you'll get. Frequently, trial and error stops after the first small benefits are seen, but this often underserves children. If there has been improvement but ADHD still impairs your child, a larger dose or different medication may be in order. You'll get more out of the medication with ongoing minor adjustments and careful comparison of the effects.

It may seem that the benefits and side effects of ADHD medication are intricately entwined, as if you can't expect one without the other. That isn't typically the case. If a medication is beneficial, that's great news; it means you're on the right track. If a medication causes persistent side effects, that's the wrong medication. You'll have more clarity in decision making when you separate the two outcomes in your mind.

Have Realistic Expectations

ADHD medications aren't miracle pills. They don't cure ADHD. They stimulate the frontal lobes to do a better job during the time any dose lasts. To implement them skillfully, you need to be aware of what they do well and what they don't.

Medications primarily improve ADHD symptoms, not executive function more generally. So distractibility, poor follow-through, fidgeting, hyperactivity, and impulsiveness should diminish. If they don't abate, the medication isn't effectively managing your child's ADHD.

Bigger-picture executive function issues, such as challenges with task management or social skills, don't directly respond to medication, but they may improve as a side benefit. For example, if your child has an easier day, his behavior at night might progress. Likewise, better focus and impulse control frequently lead to better social skills and organization. So the right medication may broadly improve life for your child. That said, when tracking the specific benefits of the medication, focus on the basic symptoms of ADHD listed in chapter 1.

Aim for Complete Symptom Control

Ideally, medication should ease your child's symptoms throughout the day. Be aware that if the effects of medication don't persist through the evening or homework, increasing the dose won't extend the effect significantly. You must either switch to a longer-acting medication or add a short-acting afternoon dose. It may be tempting to have your child take an afternoon dose only when it seems to be needed, but this often results in productivity lagging day to day, creating pressure to catch up rather than slow and steady progress.

While nonstimulant medications are effective around the clock, with stimulant medications, you'll probably face scheduling limitations. Because they can interfere with sleep, they generally provide benefits from morning to about dinnertime. If your child is taking stimulant medication, you'll want to aim to have him complete as much homework as possible during this window, while taking into account beneficial and enjoyable after-school activities.

ADHD medication isn't intended to only address problems at school. Helping your child more successfully navigate every aspect of life is important for his social development and self-esteem, so ideally he would take his medication seven days a week. If you avoid medication on weekends because of side effects, he's probably on the wrong medication or dose.

Monitor for Potential Side Effects

Statistics show that around 80 percent of children experience significant benefits from ADHD medications (Hinshaw and Scheffler 2014). The key is finding one without significant side effects. This initial process of trial and error, during which you must work closely with your child's doctor, can be emotionally grueling. But ultimately, your child should be more consistently at his best. There's no need to settle for less.

Apart from extreme reactions, monitor any apparent side effects for several days before attributing them to the medication. A child can have an off day because of a bad night's sleep, unpleasant interactions on the playground, or countless other reasons. If a medication-related pattern does become apparent, make adjustments.

Observe your child directly. Although it's safe to use stimulant medications only on school days, if you skip weekends you'll never see the effects—both pluses and minuses—yourself. And some side effects, like being emotionally withdrawn, may not be noticed in a classroom.

In monitoring for side effects, be cautious about what you communicate to your child. Frequently asking about potential side effects may convince him that he's experiencing them, and going over the extensive list of potential problems may upset him. Side effects will become apparent to you if they're present, so observe carefully and avoid communicating any anxiety.

Also track the timing of side effects. With stimulant medications, there are three patterns, each with different implications:

- Side effects at the height of the medication's effect indicate that the medication itself is the problem.

- If your child's evening behavior or emotions are more intense on days when he takes medication than they were before he started taking medication, this may indicate that the medication has worn off and created a rebound effect. The medication he's taking during the day may be fine. It's often possible to manage rebound effects by adding a small afternoon dose of the medication or by changing the formulation, including using a different version of the same medication.

- Stimulant medications cover breakfast through dinner, so your child's symptoms may return in full force at the end of the day. In addition, many children are irritable, are picky eaters, or sleep poorly, even without medication. For times when medication's effects have worn off, you'll need to focus on behavioral interventions and other nonmedication approaches. If need be, you can also consider trying a twenty-four-hour nonstimulant medication.

Monitor the Effects of Medication

To track medications, use the following table (download available) or create your own. List all benefits and any significant side effects. A medication that's a good fit will have only benefits and no side effects. Side effects indicate that it's either the wrong medication or the wrong dose, so changes are needed.

Medication Tracking

Medication:

Date started:

Time of day	Benefits (on the right track)	Side effects (on the wrong medication or dose)
Morning		
Midday		
Evening		

Ask for Teacher Feedback

Teachers should be included in the medication discussion whenever possible. They spend far more time with children at the peak of medication effects than parents do. To understand your child's classroom experience regarding both potential benefits and side effects, ask his teachers to share their observations, complete rating scales, or both.

Consider Nonstimulant Medication

As mentioned, nonstimulant medications typically aren't tried first, but they can be useful in certain situations:

- When a child doesn't experience enough benefit from stimulant medications

- When a child can't tolerate stimulant medications because of side effects

- When a child has a tic or certain other conditions that can co-occur with ADHD

- When a child needs twenty-four-hour symptom relief

Mindful Repair

A uniquely challenging stressor parents face related to ADHD has been labeled "decision-making angst" (Brinkman et al. 2009). There's ongoing pressure to decide so much, from behavioral plans to school to medication. This stress is often compounded by layers of judgment, perfectionism, the inner critic, and, all too often, not quite enough self-compassion.

There will inevitably be times when you realize that you aimed one way but life went another, or that you temporarily lost sight of your intentions. Your inner critic is likely to jump in, pointing the finger and proclaiming, *You blew it!* You may be beset by fear that you'll never solve the problem. Or you may fall back into overly familiar, painful cycles with your child or your own avoidance. Maybe you'll get annoyed at others for not following your well-thought-out plan; or maybe you'll get resentful because someone warned you that a certain choice was off target, and as it turns out, it was.

Yet any decision may not stand the test of time. The capacity to admit to a child, spouse, friend, or anyone else in your life that you were wrong, without defensiveness, takes immense courage and unflinching honesty. The difficulty of this task can be compounded by many different feelings: irritation, loneliness, anxiety, a sense of inadequacy, and on and on. Such feelings can undermine your ability to acknowledge your mistake and move forward.

This is one reason why we meditate—to see that thoughts are just thoughts and to practice letting go of assumptions, biases, and evaluations. Even with carefully weighed decisions, we simply can't be right all the time. Through practicing mindfulness, we can move beyond habitual self-judgment into something more clear-sighted as we navigate our lives.

To ease the journey, we can notice when choices go awry and then seek repair without judging ourselves or others. Say you lose track of your ADHD plan. You can just notice that and come back to it without berating yourself. Perhaps you let your mindfulness practice slip. Notice that and return to it. Maybe you don't handle a conversation as skillfully as you'd like. Just notice that and renew your intentions around communication.

With compassion, you can manage situations and remain openhearted in ways that influence what you say and do next. With less self-judgment, you're more likely to act as you intend. With less judgment of your child, you're more likely to communicate skillfully and hold on to your larger plans: *I'm angry and rattled. You're angry and rattled. I truly hope we both find some peace right now… But you still have to do your homework.* You can gather your resources, make the most skillful decision possible in the moment, and then observe the results, adapt, and try again.

Mindfulness and Compassion

Consider this situation: Your closest, most trusted friend says something hurtful to you. You're almost sure it's entirely accidental. Instinctually, you make the assumption that she didn't mean it—that she'd never intentionally be so unkind. If she approaches you afterward feeling terrible, you'd probably end up comforting and reassuring her. You'd wish her nothing but relief, even though you took the brunt of her behavior.

While we may easily extend that kind of care and compassion to a friend, we frequently don't treat ourselves as kindly. The inner critic lashes out: *You idiot! You never get anything right.* Even though we're trying our best, we heap on the abuse. But of course, we don't intentionally go out of our way to mess up our lives, no matter how it may look from the outside.

So often, we lose track of the fact that we would give someone else the benefit of the doubt but not ourselves. Whether we're on autopilot or giving a situation our full attention, we can make mistakes. Yet our desire is for happiness, and we're trying to find our way there. And really, the same goes for everyone around us: extended family members, our children's teachers and therapists, a hassled clerk or waitperson, and certainly our children. Even when we completely disagree with others or how they're acting, their intent is still happiness.

You love your child, but sometimes it may seem like he chooses to be a pain—resisting bedtime, forgetting his backpack, or whatever else gets under your skin. When you're caught up in the struggle of trying to keep him on track, frustration may sometimes mask your larger wish for his well-being. He's seeking happiness and, as happens to everyone, something has gotten in the way. It can, unfortunately, be easy to lose track of his side of the story.

You may wonder how you can make strong decisions, protect yourself, and still acknowledge others' perspectives. You may feel vulnerable when extending compassion to both yourself and others, as if you are in some way condoning their perhaps inappropriate actions. It can feel much easier and often safer to defend, withdraw, or shut others out. But if you fall back on these kinds of reactions repeatedly, it will affect both you and those around you. Compassion-focused mindfulness practices can guide you past these habitual barriers. With effort and repetition, it's possible to hardwire new neural pathways that reinforce compassion in interactions with yourself, your child, and the world.

Practice: Loving-Kindness Meditation

(Audio download available.) In this compassion practice, there's no aim to force anything to happen. You cannot will yourself into particular feelings toward yourself or anyone else. Rather, the practice is simply to remind yourself that you deserve happiness and ease—no more and no less than anyone else—and that the same goes for your child, your family, your friends, your neighbors, and everyone else in the world. Everyone is driven by an inner desire to avoid suffering and find a measure of peace. In this practice, that universal aspect of the human condition is the focus of attention.

> *Find a comfortable, stable position, either seated or lying down, and observe several breaths. Notice how you're feeling while letting go of striving or effort to feel otherwise. You cannot force yourself to feel relaxed, nonjudgmental, or anything else in particular. Let yourself simply feel whatever you feel.*

Next, picture your child. Imagine what you most wish for him. This unbounded affection, deeper than any surface emotions, has traditionally been encompassed within four phrases: "May you be happy. May you be healthy. May you feel safe. May you live your life with ease." Use these phrases or any that capture your deepest wishes, and silently repeat them at a comfortable pace, timed to your breathing.

Continue repeating these wishes for your child, reminding yourself of your deepest intentions: "May you be happy. May you be healthy. May you feel safe. May you live your life with ease."

After several minutes, move on to yourself. Your inner critic may resist. Yet in spite of all your seeming mistakes, you have the same rights as anyone: "May I be happy. May I be healthy. May I feel safe. May I live my life with ease." Without any sort of demand, offer yourself the same wishes for well-being you extended to your child.

After several minutes, imagine a close friend or someone unconditionally supportive, a person for whom you have almost entirely positive feelings. This person also desires happiness, whether going through a stretch of relative ease or more acutely in need of your emotional support. If no one comes to mind, that's fine and quite common; just continue with the practice for yourself.

After a few minutes have passed, move on to a neutral person, someone you see around but don't really know—maybe someone at a local store or gas station, or who works nearby. Extend the same wishes to this neutral person without judging whatever you actually feel or aiming to push yourself. You're simply paying attention in this way.

Now think of a difficult person—not the most difficult, but someone you've disagreed with in a smaller way. Your perspectives differ and you must firmly take care of yourself, yet this difficult person's actions are also driven by a wish for happiness. If this person found relief from his own suffering, it's likely that his behavior would change. If it's easier, include yourself: "May we both be happy. May we both be healthy. May we both feel safe. May we both live our lives with ease."

Next, picture your entire family for a while: "May all of us be happy. May all of us be healthy. May all of us feel safe. May we all live our lives with ease."

Finally, if you like, extend the same wishes to everyone in this world. In an unforced way, send this compassionate wish for well-being to anyone you imagine, anywhere.

As this practice becomes comfortable for you, you can use it to combat everyday stress. If you feel unmoored, lost, or pulled in different directions, take a moment to wish yourself peace, just as you'd comfort a friend. If your child frustrates you and you lose your temper, briefly practice this meditation for his sake and your own. Remind yourself of your child's desire for happiness and your own wishes for the same, whatever he may have done.

Action Plan: Coordinating Treatment Decisions

While the focus of this chapter is medication, in reality you're always making decisions about your child and his ADHD care. You decide how to act and speak, how to manage situations and schedules, and countless other details. Stress, uncertainty, and many other challenges will impact the process. Take care of yourself, continue your mindfulness practice, seek out objective information, and then make the most well-informed decision you can in any given moment.

☐ Practice bringing mindfulness to decision making around choices about medication or other aspects of your child's ADHD care.

☐ Whatever choice you make in regard to medication or other interventions, make a note on your calendar to assess its outcome periodically.

☐ If your child is just starting on ADHD medication or changing medication, assess his response often and adjust as needed to optimize the benefits of medication:

    ☐ Monitor for improvement in specific ADHD symptoms.

    ☐ Seek feedback from your child's teachers.

    ☐ Change the medication or dose as needed to eliminate side effects.

    ☐ Find a medication or combination of medications that eases symptoms until homework and after-school activities are completed.

☐ Once medications start working, reassess other interventions. Behavioral and educational plans that didn't work well in the past may be more successful once your child can better self-regulate.

☐ Practice loving-kindness meditation on a regular basis—perhaps once a day for the first week—and notice how it affects difficult encounters and decisions.

Chapter 10

Creating Routines That Work

Read this chapter to...

- See how ADHD impacts everyday routines

- Understand how healthy habits influence ADHD

- Establish household routines that promote well-being and independence

- Stay on track when you become hooked by something unsettling and feel an urge to react

You set out with the best intentions for your child. Perhaps you've vowed to stay calm while discussing another homework assignment not handed in. Then your child offers a pile of disjointed excuses; you fall back into that pedantic, nagging tone you vowed never to use again, and your child reacts in kind. You are emphatically, viscerally hooked.

Or maybe your child gets off the bus and conversation zings along as she tells you about how much fun she had that day. Then you say, "That's great! Let's get your homework done and then we can play," and a pall drops over her. You fear that anything you say next may trigger an explosion. She's hooked—unsettled and off-balance, ready for anything but a reasoned, rational talk about your plan.

You know that how you respond will influence what happens next, yet an emotional shock wave is sweeping through your mind and body. You get hooked despite understanding that managing your child's ADHD, and parenting in general, relies on compassion, respectful communication, and acting in alignment with your intentions. Your child may sense the fact that you're hooked and become worried and off balance herself. Without awareness of these common patterns, your intentions and carefully constructed plans can fall by the wayside—all in a single moment.

ADHD and Everyday Life

Getting hooked is inevitable in life, perhaps especially in a household living with ADHD. Everyday routines are anything but routine. You may stew about why your child resists bedtime night after night despite being exhausted; or you may wonder why, after so many years, getting out the door in the morning is still such a fraught experience. When you're caught up in the battle, your logical brain knows it's wiser not to say anything to escalate the situation, but you do. Curses, hooked again.

Because of executive function issues, ADHD inherently involves difficulty in establishing and maintaining routines. From getting out the door to getting to bed and everything in between, this places increased demands on parents. And when parents feel stressed, emotionally triggered, or otherwise overwhelmed, they often drift still further away from the touchstone of everyday routine.

Yet consistent routines make daily life simpler, for both parents and children with ADHD. In fact, family routines have been linked to childhood happiness and well-being (Muniz, Silver, and Stein 2014). Plus, any habit established in early childhood is more likely to persist into adolescence. It's far easier to guide young children toward developing healthy habits around sleep, technology, nutrition, or exercise than to convince a media-addled, sleep-deprived teen to make changes. In all these ways and more, establishing effective routines will build the exact skills your child needs to outgrow the daily turmoil often caused by ADHD.

Many lifestyle-related choices related to routines can have an impact on ADHD. Research suggests that good nutrition, exercise, and sleep can improve ADHD. Mindfulness does as well, and chapter 11 will explore how you can share mindfulness with your child. Yet establishing healthier habits in all of these areas is harder when a child has ADHD. Therefore, this chapter offers guidance on establishing key routines to support your child in these areas and help your household run more smoothly.

First Things First: The Importance of a Morning Routine

Mornings can feel pressured in any household with children. When a child has difficulties with hyperactivity, impulsiveness, distractibility, managing time, prioritizing, or keeping track of details, mornings often become an ongoing crisis. For children taking stimulant medication, the effects haven't kicked in yet. And parents, before they're fully awake, may more easily end up arguing with their children while herding them out the door. This can cast a pall on the entire day.

To turn things around, make sure your child's morning routine is, well, routine. Here are some pointers:

- Write down a step-by-step routine or create a picture chart. Even when children with ADHD can recite a plan verbatim, in the heat of the moment they'll lose track of the details. Encourage your child to check the list frequently as she gets ready so she stays on track. Following such lists is a vital skill that will be useful to her throughout life.

- Keep the list short. If any tasks can be moved to the evening before, such as showering, packing a lunch, or organizing her backpack, do so. In the short term, consider eliminating anything unnecessary, like making the bed. As the initial routine becomes habit, some of those tasks can be moved to the morning and incorporated into the list. For now, focus on what absolutely must happen. Initially, the list might look like this:

  · Get dressed

- Eat

- Brush your teeth and hair

- Get your backpack

- Leave the house in time to catch the bus

- Mandate that the list be completed both by a certain time and before playing, building in at least fifteen minutes before your child actually has to leave. If she needs to be out the door at 8:00, set 7:45 as the goal. Emphasize the fact that she'll have a few minutes for play or downtime if she completes the list on time.

- If the routine seems to be within your child's capabilities but she has difficulty following it, tie it to a reward system. Award a point for finishing on time while sustaining a good attitude.

Q&A

Q: My child seems to go through her routine slowly no matter what I do. How can I make her move faster?

A: Many children with ADHD have their own mental pace and can't be forced into moving more quickly. Setting up routines and checklists helps with efficiency, as does eliminating excess detail from a routine when possible, like setting out clothes at bedtime instead of deciding in the morning. But sometimes all you can do is allot more time, perhaps setting the alarm earlier. You can also look out for "mental oobleck." Oobleck is a liquid that rapidly turns solid under pressure. Some people with ADHD describe something similar cognitively: pressure leads them to move slower, get flustered, and make mistakes. In that case, easing off or engaging your child in a brief mindfulness practice may lead to quicker task completion.

Eating and Exercise

Because ADHD is a disorder of self-regulation, it shouldn't be surprising that it affects eating. Distracted and impulsive eating leads to poor eating habits in general, and the chronic stress associated with ADHD also affects choices about food. Poor time management is another problem, leading to missed meals that cause kids to make pressured, poor food choices later, as one example. And while mealtime resistance to certain foods is common among all children, the emotional reactivity of those with ADHD sends it to a new level, sometimes causing parents to give up on a well-rounded diet for their child. Unfortunately, a growing body of research links ADHD and obesity (Dempsey, Dyehouse, and Schafer 2011).

Establishing a few key routines around eating can be very helpful. For example, eating meals together as a family has been correlated with healthier eating habits, decreased risk of eating disorders, better grades, and reduced behavioral issues in teens (Fiese and Schwartz 2008). Set a time to sit down for dinner together, and at that time, turn off the TV and smartphones and enjoy the meal and each other's company.

Mindful eating also has potential benefits. Revisit the mindful eating practice in chapter 1 and consider how you can model more conscious eating habits for your child. Use books like *No Ordinary Apple* by Sara Marlowe (2013) to guide your child in mindful eating.

Also be aware that recent studies indicate that certain dietary approaches may have a positive impact ADHD:

- Deficits of iron and possibly zinc have been linked to ADHD symptoms in some studies (Millichap and Yee 2012). Screening for iron deficiency is routine in the United States, so ask your child's pediatrician about her iron status. Zinc isn't typically measured (yet also hasn't been as clearly linked to ADHD). Mineral deficiencies are unlikely in the modern diet; still, for a picky eater you may want to consider a multivitamin that contains both iron and zinc.

- Omega-3 fatty acids, such as in fish oil, have shown potential benefits (Bloch and Qawasmi 2011). The jury is still out, so they aren't yet generally recommended for children. If you'd like to try increasing your child's intake, dietary sources like seafood are a good start. It's probably best to consult with your child's pediatrician before using omega-3 supplements in order to determine appropriate amounts.

- Food dyes may increase ADHD symptoms in some children (Millichap and Yee 2012). These dyes don't cause ADHD, and they're present only in blatantly unhealthy foods. If your child gets wound up after eating or drinking neon-colored products, avoid them in the future.

- As a side note, there is no evidence that gluten-free or other elimination diets impact ADHD.

Consistent exercise has also been shown to benefit ADHD (Halperin, Berwid, and O'Neill 2014). Like many parents, you may find that your child's moods and behaviors are better after an active day. Be sure to schedule exercise, whether through play or sports, including during cold weather. Also advocate for opportunities for exercise at school and ask teachers and other school personnel to avoid punishments that keep your child out of gym or recess. You might use the exercise "Decluttering Your Life," from chapter 3, to prioritize activities that make exercise a regular part of your child's day-to-day life.

Perchance to Sleep

A child with ADHD lies down at night. All external distractions drop away in the dark, quiet room. Alone with her busy mind, her thoughts about the day swirl around and mix with the physical restlessness of ADHD. Maybe she experiences a hint of fear or gets bored.

The most appealing path for her at that moment is to find something engaging to do. So she jumps on the bed, watches television, runs downstairs, or asks for yet another glass of water. But this just further activates her mind and stimulates her body. By her very nature, she needs everything to be perfectly aligned in order to fall asleep, yet she ends up doing everything possible to stay awake.

Most every parent has experienced the claustrophobic fugue that envelops the room while trying to convince a child to lie down and stay still long enough to fall asleep. You may console, cajole, beg, or plead, but your child won't be compelled by once again hearing how important sleep is for health and well-being. She may pop out of bed repeatedly, refuse to let go of your neck, or turn on the light the moment you step away.

Bedtime epitomizes all the demands and challenges inherent to parenting. You may remain calm on the outside while churning internally, and you may muster your resources, only to discover that you can't control everything after all. Yet helping your child sleep well is essential, both in the moment and in the long run. Adults with ADHD often report having sleep problems, so helping your child establish good sleep habits now may solidify into a lifetime of benefits.

It's also crucial for your own self-care. If your child regularly pushes against night-time limits, you'll become chronically exhausted. This makes it harder for you to stick to routines, including those around sleep, so the cycle continues.

At least 40 percent of children with ADHD have sleep disturbances, ranging from difficulty falling asleep to disrupted sleep (Barkley 2014). However, one analysis showed that almost any sleep plan can be effective, with a catch: the plan must be implemented consistently (Mindell et al. 2006). Here's what the research says about healthy sleep.

Establish a Consistent Sleep Schedule

Going to bed at the same time every day can help reset your child's internal clock and promote good sleep. Most children benefit from having a consistent bedtime and sticking to it. And like all people, they have what's called a sleep window—a time at which they fall asleep most easily as their internal clock, or circadian rhythm, readies the body for sleep.

Putting your child to bed too early will make it challenging for her to fall asleep. But if you set a bedtime that's too late, your child will miss her sleep window and potentially become restless again. With an appropriate bedtime, your child should be putting her head on the pillow as her body slows. If her sleep window is unclear, monitor her over time to notice when she slows even a little at night.

Whatever bedtime you decide upon, set an alarm if you tend to lose track of time yourself.

Establish a Relaxing Bedtime Routine.

Once you've decided upon a bedtime, create a bedtime routine for slowing down, starting about an hour earlier than you've decided it's time for lights out. Each night, go through the same routine of calming activities, such as showering or bathing, playing a quiet game, and then reading. Avoid horsing around or any stimulating activity that revs up the body or mind, including most forms of media (discussed in detail later in this chapter). Exercising early in the day can promote sleep at night, but near bedtime it tends to be too stimulating.

Offering a choice between reading and sleeping is a great way to encourage a life-time habit: "Bedtime is at 8:00, but you can read until 8:30." It's one of the healthiest nighttime choices children can make.

If your child wakes and gets out of bed, put her back in bed without discussion. Don't let bedtime struggles become a source of attention. If she needs something, provide it with minimal conversation. If the only thing she "needs" is to avoid staying in bed, direct her firmly and dispassionately to lie down again. And if sleep issues are at the top of your behavioral triage list, increase her motivation by tying compliance with her nighttime routine, and staying in bed, to her reward system.

Encourage Sustainable Sleep Associations

Both when falling asleep and while cycling through light sleep several times during the night, your child may consciously or unconsciously reach for a comforting object (like a stuffed toy) or check to see whether you're there; these are called *sleep associations*. A vital part of a bedtime routine is creating sustainable sleep associations that allow your child to settle herself and fall back into deep sleep on her own.

Whenever possible, avoid becoming a sleep association yourself. Be soothing and present through her bedtime routine, then step away so she doesn't come to rely upon you for sleep—or so you don't become a distraction from sleep. Instead, make your child's bedroom and bed a space in which she feels safe and comfortable, with stuffed animals or other soft toys, pictures, or whatever else soothes her.

If you've already become part of what your child needs to fall asleep, gradually reduce your presence. To move your child out of your bed or yourself out of her bedroom, pick a start date. Consider fading the physical routine, perhaps sitting near her bed, then moving toward the door gradually over several weeks. Take the same approach with checking on your child as she's falling asleep, first returning after five minutes, then after ten, and so on. With any of these approaches, anticipate several weeks of difficulty as you change the rules.

Monitor for Anxiety

If fearfulness or anxiety is undermining your child's sleep, discuss this with your child's pediatrician or therapist. There are many ways to manage anxiety. The practice of mindfulness is one, and in the next chapter you'll find guidance on how to introduce mindfulness to your child.

If sleep issues persist after you've tried all of the approaches in the previous sections and given them a chance to work, consult your child's health-care provider. If your child is taking a stimulant medication, changing the medication, adjusting the dose, or switching to a nonstimulant option may help. Since children with ADHD are at risk for sleep disorders, discuss persistent concerns with your pediatrician. You might also ask about having your child take melatonin on a trial basis.

Incorporate Meditation or Relaxation Exercises

Many children need to learn how to divert attention from feelings of restlessness or busy thoughts long enough to settle down for sleep. Relaxation exercises of any kind may be useful. One possibility is the following mindfulness practice, the body scan, which involves focusing attention on the body, part by part. Although mindfulness typically builds alertness, around bedtime it may promote sleep.

Practice: Body Scan Meditation

The instructions below are intended for your own use. (A downloadable guided audio version is available, as are both audio and written instructions for guiding younger children in the body scan.) When doing this meditation, remember that, as always, there's no need to strive to make anything happen. Simply observe what you find and practice letting things be for a while. When something uncomfortable grabs your attention, like pain or an itch, observe it first and see if it changes. If you find you need to address it, that's fine. Noticing that, pause and make an adjustment. In this way, the body scan provides an opportunity to practice responsiveness.

Begin by lying down or sitting in a comfortable chair. If lying down, let your arms and legs relax and fall to the sides; if seated, find a balanced and stable position.

Take a few moments to notice sensations of breathing.

Draw your attention to your feet. Notice the pressure of your feet against the floor or bed, the temperature, comfort or discomfort, itches, or anything else. Expect your mind to wander, and when it does, return your attention to your feet without judging yourself or giving yourself a hard time. Let your attention rest with your feet in this way for a few minutes.

Move attention to your lower legs. You might feel the touch of clothing or a blanket, and you might feel nothing at all. Sustain your attention without rigidly exhausting yourself. Whatever you experience, that's what you're supposed to feel right now.

After a few minutes, shift attention to your upper legs, observing them in the same way.

Pacing yourself, turn this same kind of attention to your abdomen and then to your chest. Notice physical sensations, such as breathing, internal feelings like hunger or fullness, and the resonance of any emotions—physical manifestations of happiness, sadness, tension, anger, feeling open or closed, and so on.

Continue turning attention to the rest of your body in the same way, spending several minutes each on your back, then your hands, then your arms. Then bring attention to your neck and shoulders, releasing tension when you're able without fighting what remains.

Finally, bring attention to your face and head, noticing expressions and reflections of emotions that occur around your mouth and eyes in particular.

Whether you feel relaxed or tense, restless or invigorated, pause before concluding. Take a moment of stillness, and then, with intention, choose when to move on with your day.

Using Technology or Being Used by It?

Screens—televisions, computers, smartphones, tablets, and all the rest—have become part of the framework of our culture. They're ubiquitous and engaging and can be useful tools for efficiency, but they have potential downsides as well. For a modern parent, guiding children around the use of technology is as important as teaching them to eat well and exercise.

Many children with ADHD have difficulty self-monitoring around technology. They lose track of time, hyperfocus, prioritize poorly, and strain to transition attention. On their own, they spend up to twice as much time in front of screens as their peers do (Mazurek and Engelhardt 2013).

In essence, video games and the Internet create a perfect storm around ADHD. A child struggles to stay engaged and gets easily bored because of his brain wiring. Craving novelty, he finds a medium that grabs hold and does not let go. This unique interaction between screens and ADHD sets up trouble when children have unfettered access.

Excessive media time has been linked with attention and behavior problems, obesity, academic struggles, drinking, smoking and a host of other undesirable outcomes. In addition, television may have the potential to disrupt language development (Chonchaiya and Pruksananonda 2008) and parent-child interactions (Courage et al. 2010; Kirkorian et al. 2009). Just because screen time is easy, and just because kids enjoy it, doesn't mean it should take over their childhood.

In fact, studies suggest that attention worsens as screen time grows (Johnson et al. 2007; Swing et al. 2010). The average video game or show doesn't encourage sustained focus but instead emphasizes rapid shifting of attention amidst continual action. This influences child development whether we want it to or not, and often parallels the troubles associated with ADHD. Consider the following potential risks associated with ADHD versus those associated with excessive exposure to media:

Risks Associated with ADHD	Risks Associated with Media
Aggressive behavior	Aggressive behavior
Academic problems	Academic problems
Attention problems	Attention problems
Obesity or poor eating habits	Obesity or poor eating habits
Sleep problems	Sleep problems

Technology, Productivity, and Education

Technology can increase efficiency, but organization and planning are necessary for that to happen. For anyone with executive function issues, technology frequently morphs into yet another source of distraction and scattered, impulsive interactions that consume time and energy.

As noted above, screen time may even impair attention and executive function. In one study, skills were measured after young children viewed just nine minutes of either a popular cartoon or a slower-paced public television program (Lillard and Peterson 2011). Children showed decreased executive function only after the fast-paced cartoon. And in the real world, who stops after only nine minutes? Other studies correlate increasing hours of screen time with decreasing ability to focus (Johnson et al. 2007; Swing et al. 2010).

In education, the cart has gotten far ahead of the horse. Schools are increasingly investing in tablets and software programs, yet research hasn't yet shown that kids learn well from computers. Meanwhile, computers have become so ubiquitous that many kids get bored with educational games. Videos and video games may augment certain aspects of learning at home and at school, but only when carefully selected.

Of course, a computer program can never substitute for individualized attention and feedback from a skilled teacher. For children with ADHD, sitting in front of a screen instead of interacting with a person allows for distracted, off-task time without adult redirection. Far more evidence backs the effectiveness of reading with children over videos or many other "educational" products (Reach Out and Read 2014).

To effectively harness the power of technology without incurring the downsides, children and teens need adult monitoring. Otherwise an Internet search on a topic can easily turn into two hours watching videos, or the intent to use an app for organization can lead to texting, playing games, and a long string of activities other than getting organized.

Why Media Management Matters

Media is a product meant to hold our attention. A riveting video game or show is specifically designed not to have a clean end point. It doesn't pause to remind kids to do their homework or get outside and play. Lots of thought goes into grabbing kids and keeping them engaged.

Video games and shows are cotton candy for the mind; while a little might be fine, it isn't a good idea to consume too much of it too often. Yet it can be tempting to shrug off the issue for many reasons. Screens provide mindless fun and often serve as a harmless distraction for kids while parents get things done. But that doesn't make them benign, and for most children, strong parental oversight is necessary for a healthy relationship with technology.

While some children do fine regardless of choices made around screen time, hundreds of studies document ill effects from media exposure (for example, Christakis et al. 2004; Nunez-Smith et al. 2010). Children with ADHD are especially at risk because of their problems with self-regulation. One of the most important decisions you can make as a parent is to enforce healthy habits around screens.

Managing media use has been shown to have immediate benefits. In one study, preschoolers' sleep improved after parents were shown a simple education program around using media with their children (Garrison and Christakis 2012). In another study, aggressive behavior decreased after reducing use of television, videos, and video games (Robinson et al. 2001). Of course, screen time also takes up time that could be spent on healthier activities. Managing media use often allows children to blossom in other parts of life.

Creating Healthier Media Habits

For kids and parents alike, screens and technology entertain, educate, and keep us connected with loved ones. But much of how we use our devices is driven by the industry itself, through everything from marketing to placing televisions and computers everywhere we look. Instead of mindlessly following along, we can all benefit from pausing to consider how technology is serving us. So in addition to considering direct effects on your child, look at how media use—your own and your child's—affects family time. Then proactively decide how you want to use technology in your home.

Step out of autopilot. Strong parental involvement in shaping kids' media habits has been correlated with physical, academic, social, and emotional benefits (Gentile et al. 2014). Children shouldn't consume media without guidance any more than they should be permitted to eat fast food and candy all day long. Without dwelling on how your family related to media in the past, take the following commonsense steps to manage media for your child and yourself:

- **Set daily limits.** Again, revisit the exercise "Decluttering Your Life," from chapter 3. Schedule everything that's required and everything you value as a family, then confine possible screen time to the free time remaining, with a maximum of one to two hours daily.

- **Monitor content.** The media industry itself created the various age rating systems on labels, so they lack intrinsic value. Seek out neutral sources of information such as Common Sense Media (https://www.commonsensemedia.org). To avoid debate, tell your child that these independent guides will determine what they can see.

- **Monitor Internet use.** Keep screens in common areas of the house when possible—though as devices get smaller and more mobile this becomes an increasing challenge. Young children can't monitor themselves well enough to have unfettered access to everything on the Internet. Don't give them their own devices until they seem ready to use them appropriately, and when they're accessing the Internet, either supervise them or use content filters.

- **Avoid marketing when possible.** Emphasize DVDs and other forms of media that don't include commercials. Unfortunately, much marketing is unavoidable, so explain to your child how it works and its intentions. For both children and adults, this awareness can help undermine the influence of marketing.

- **Model appropriate behavior.** Monitor how much time you spend in front of a screen when you could be interacting with your family. Keep track of how often checking your phone interrupts playtime or mealtime. Demonstrate to your child that she comes first.

- **Set a media bedtime for the household.** Avoiding screens for a solid hour before bedtime promotes healthy sleep (Stony Brook University 2014). Set a time for turning off phones, laptops, and other devices and stick to it. One simple way to encourage a nightly break from technology is to create a central charging station, out of bedrooms, for everyone to use.

- **Teach teens to shut off distractions.** Many teens do their homework on a computer, juggling assignments with social media and entertaining websites. Although this is less than ideal, most adolescents with strong executive function get by. But kids with ADHD end up spending far more time on the distractions. Doing homework during scheduled times when e-mail and social media are off—an approach some business executives now take in their jobs—increases productivity. You can also install applications and programs that prompt users to shut off distracting content on the computer when needed.

- **Teach your child to use technology skillfully.** Guide your child in making the most of technology with electronic to-do lists, calendars, alarms, and other organizational programs. Discuss and monitor Internet searches, and consider posting a reminder on the edge of the screen about what topic is being explored. When your child begins to use a new software program or app, supervise her and provide guidance on how to get the most out of it.

- **Add a behavioral component to your child's media plan.** Make screen time contingent on appropriate behavior or completion of homework. One particularly useful tool for handling media battles is to tie tomorrow's time to today's behavior: "Your baseline is forty-five minutes daily, but if you quit watching without arguing today, you get an extra fifteen minutes tomorrow."

- **Discuss Internet and social media use.** From an early age, build awareness of the potential for any electronic message or posting to be either misinterpreted or broadcast to the numerous people. Children and teens, particularly those with ADHD, often lack foresight and act impulsively. The WAIT acronym, outlined in the accompanying text box, can be helpful.

Pause Before Send

Tristan Gorrindo, a child and adolescent psychiatrist at Massachusetts General Hospital, has created a useful acronym for anyone using social media (Gorrindo 2010).

W = Wide audience: *Would I say this in front of a school assembly?*

A = Affect, or mood: *Am I in a good emotional place right now?*

I = Intent: *Might what I mean be misunderstood?*

T = Today: *Does this need to be posted or sent right away? Would there be benefit to reevaluating tomorrow?*

Releasing Hooks

Creating more effective and consistent routines can go a long way toward decreasing how often you and your child get hooked. They create a platform for success. Even so, you will get hooked sometimes. Despite everything we try, all of us get hooked at times. Your child may generally comply with her bedtime routine and sleep well, but sometimes you will hear that dreaded footstep on the stairs in the middle of the night and feel the visceral reaction of being hooked once again.

Being hooked tends to trigger the mental habits outlined in chapter 7: grasping, aversion, restlessness, self-doubt, and feeling overwhelmed. On a behavioral level, you might seek relief by drinking, yelling, overeating, withdrawing, or in countless other ways. Yet these habits tend to make things harder, not easier, in the long run.

Of course, some methods of seeking relief can be useful. If doing something like going for a run makes you feel better, go for it. But if running becomes a compulsion, it probably isn't entirely beneficial. Or perhaps you choose to brainstorm solutions to whatever hooked you. If you can do so creatively and in an intentional way, that's great. But spending two or three hours worrying and hashing over the same possible responses again and again in the middle of the night won't be useful.

The compulsion to take action in response to being hooked is often based on an assumption, perhaps unconscious, that when we feel unsettled, we need an immediate solution. There can be a false sense that because something, perhaps a drink or a chocolate bar, alleviates our pain in the moment, it will do so indefinitely. This can create a vicious cycle: we pursue temporary solace, but the uneasiness inevitably returns because we haven't addressed the root cause, so we take the same way out again and again.

Although the idea that an immediate solution exists for every difficulty may seem comforting, it actually amplifies our distress. Life tends to be messy. Yes, sometimes there are clear solutions to problems: *I'm thirsty, so I'm getting a glass of water.* But often there's nothing useful we can say or do in the moment, but we say or do something anyway. And in many cases, it's only after the fact that we become aware that we were hooked and reacted in ways we wish we hadn't: *I promised I'd walk away and calm myself next time, but I didn't.*

This can be a painful realization and may become a new hook. Remind yourself that the experience of getting hooked is a universal difficulty. When it happens, don't fight the hook; that will only set it in deeper.

Getting Unhooked

It can be hard to acknowledge discomfort and not take action. But refraining in this way may allow the sensation to run its course without us adding anything to it: *I'm hooked, and what makes most sense is to remain aware of my distress while I get on with my day.* Sometimes there is nothing more useful we can do. So whenever you recognize that you've been hooked, practice pausing. Instead of fighting against it, relax as best as you can. Refrain, even if for only a moment, from falling back on habitual reactions.

This type of intentional pause doesn't mean becoming passive. In fact, noticing that you've been hooked and what has hooked you may help you act more decisively. For example, say you're embroiled in yet another argument with your child over bedtime and, exhausted yourself, you just want to capitulate. Then, as you pause, you realize that, in spite of your desire to give in, ultimately you can stay true to your child's new routine and your intentions in establishing it.

Notice any urge to banish the sensation of being hooked through sheer effort alone. Instead, observe what's occurring in your body and in your mind. Remember the Serenity Prayer and seek the courage to change the things you can, the ability to accept the things you cannot change, and the wisdom to tell the difference.

As you turn your attention to noticing getting hooked, that may set another hook: *I blew it! I can't believe I got hooked again!* Remind yourself that, like everyone else, you're doing your best, and extend compassion to yourself. Also return to your mindfulness practice. Noticing, pausing, and realigning yourself with your intentions creates an opportunity to respond in new ways.

Working with Hooks

During any mindfulness practice, physical sensations show up, whether an aching knee, an itch, or an urge to fidget. Mental sensations also grab hold: compiling to-do lists, mulling over problems, or rehashing conversations. More amorphous mental and emotional states also arise: impatience, boredom, restlessness... All can be unpleasant, and often there is nothing useful to be done. In this way, mindfulness meditation is an avenue to developing a greater ability to experience discomfort without immediately reacting and compounding the situation.

On a literal level, when you're sitting in meditation, you're safe. If your hair is on fire, put it out; but for anything less, there is space to observe before acting. When you notice discomfort and other hooks and the accompanying urge to react, you have an opportunity to practice letting go instead.

Even when logic suggests there is nothing to be done, that perspective is hard to sustain when you're hooked. But you can practice noticing the tightness, the heat, and the urge to act while letting things be, at least for a moment. You can still take care of yourself, take action, and fix whatever needs fixing when that's possible. But sometimes you may benefit from simply observing what's happening without adding anything else to your experience.

Whenever you notice that you're hooked, pause and aim yourself toward the most skillful response available to you right then. Many forms of discomfort pass if we leave them alone, and many aren't fully under our control. If you have an itch, it's probably okay to scratch. With other hooks—other kinds of itches—your best option may be to simply refrain from irritating things further, for a moment accepting the discomfort just as it is.

Practice: Releasing the Hook

According to esteemed author and mindfulness teacher Pema Chödrön (2006), the following four Rs can make working with hooks easier. Consider this to be an informal, in-the-moment mindfulness practice that you can use anytime you notice that you're hooked:

- **Recognize** when you're feeling hooked.

- **Refrain** from acting on the sensation.

- **Relax** when you notice yourself tensing or getting restless.

- **Resolve** to keep working on breaking the cycle—old habits die hard.

Action Plan: Establishing and Sustaining Daily Routines

Nothing prompts feelings of uncertainty and getting hooked more than parenting. We care about the well-being of our children more than anything, but there's only so much we can do. You can set up highly effective routines and try to anticipate everything, but your child will still have her own mind, make her own choices, and experience random events. When you notice yourself getting hooked and then pause and refrain from habitual reactions, you can more easily stick to your intentions throughout life, including setting up healthy routines for your child.

- [ ] When building any routine for your child, keep in mind her executive function abilities. Create a routine that meets her where she is in her development, not based on her calendar age.

- [ ] Use the triage approach, selecting a recurring activity in everyday life that could benefit from creating a new routine as outlined in this chapter. (See chapter 8 for homework routines.)

- [ ] For any routine, externalize the system with written or picture lists, alarms, and reminders.

- [ ] Tie the new routine to a reward system to encourage success.

- [ ] If it remains difficult to establish important routines, consult with a professional.

- [ ] Notice when you become hooked in ways that make routines more stressful or less successful and consider using Pema Chödrön's four Rs practice.

- [ ] Practice mindfulness and, whenever you lose touch with your daily practice, readjust and come back. Bring some focus to traits you aim to develop and offer back to your child: wisdom, calm, strength, humor, or whatever fits for you. Write these traits below:

_____

_____

_____

Chapter 11

Mindfulness for Children

Read this chapter to...

- See what research says about adults and children who practice mindfulness

- Initiate a mindfulness practice with your child

- Sustain mindfulness practice both for yourself and for your family

As discussed shortly, exciting research suggests that anyone can improve attention by practicing mindfulness. Unsurprisingly, when people hear that attention is trainable in that way, they often wonder about using meditation to treat ADHD. As in much of life, the situation isn't that simple. ADHD and mindfulness both affect far more than attention. Interestingly, the processes involved in ADHD and mindfulness uniquely mirror each other. ADHD is characterized by difficulties with executive function, not just attention, and mindfulness is an avenue to developing a variety of interrelated cognitive skills, not just attention.

As it turns out, training in mindfulness can be profoundly beneficial not only for children's ADHD, but for their entire future. Like parents, children are often stressed, overwhelmed, or burned out, particularly if they have ADHD. That affects how they live and relate to the world. Mindfulness can ease these difficulties for children, just as it can for adults.

Mindfulness Research in Adults and Children

The number of research papers dedicated to mindfulness has increased exponentially for several decades, and the results consistently point to the same exceptional fact: we have the capacity to build cognitive traits that advance both physical and mental health. Mindfulness benefits everything from stress and anxiety to depression, sometimes after as little as a week of practice. And perhaps because chronic stress exacerbates most medical disorders, mindfulness can be helpful for conditions ranging from psoriasis and rheumatoid arthritis to chronic pain and cancer (Carlson 2012).

As mentioned, research even shows that the brain responds to mindfulness training with physical changes. Thinning of the brain's outer surface has been described as an inevitable part of aging, yet one Harvard study showed that long-term meditators experienced no loss (Lazar et al. 2005). Studies have shown that some areas of the brain, including areas related to emotion regulation, grew during an eight-week mindfulness program (Singleton et al. 2014). And studies involving both imaging and patterns of activation in the brain have shown alterations correlating with greater emotional control, well-being, and happiness (Davidson et al. 2003; Lazar et al. 2005).

While research in children isn't as extensive as that for adults, it has generally shown the same benefits, with improvements around stress, attention, and executive function, in addition to other behavioral measures. In one UCLA study, children who lagged behind their peers in executive function at the start of a mindfulness program experienced larger gains than their classmates (Flook et al. 2010).

Children may also engage in more acts of compassion after mindfulness practice. In one study (Flook et al. 2014), preschool children were asked to give stickers to kids in a group that included children they identified as liking, not liking, or not knowing. Unsurprisingly, initially most were given to friends. After participating in a mindfulness program, the same children handed out the stickers more evenly.

Research is now zeroing in on mindfulness and ADHD. In one study, both adolescents with ADHD and their parents reported decreased stress levels and fewer ADHD symptoms after a mindfulness program (Haydicky et al. 2013). Mindfulness has been correlated with improvements similar to those with medication for several aspects of attention and cognition (Schoenberg et al. 2014). And traits inherent to ADHD, such as impulsiveness and emotional reactivity, respond to mindfulness practice, as do some aspects of executive function (Flook et al. 2010).

For kids with ADHD, the potential for mindfulness ranges from improved focus and executive function to greater general well-being. Therefore, future directions for ADHD care may increasingly incorporate approaches based in mindfulness. After all, if you train attention with mindfulness, attention improves. This alone is an incredible approach through which anyone, with or without ADHD, can benefit.

Still, in fairness, nothing published to date suggests that mindfulness, on its own, can overcome the genetics of ADHD. Mindfulness aims toward a larger set of traits, including responsiveness, flexible thinking, and compassion. With ADHD, it supports improved resilience and a capacity to resolutely manage the challenges of life. For all of these reasons and more, mindfulness profoundly affects the lives of families who commit to practicing it together.

Translating Mindfulness for Children

Based on your work with this book, you're now aware of how mindfulness supports you and your family. You may be eager to introduce mindfulness to your child. Rest assured that in taking the time to work on your own mindfulness, you've already started. Children are hardwired to learn from adults, so building your own awareness, responsiveness, flexible thinking, and compassion creates an example for your child. The single most vital step toward teaching your child mindfulness is living it.

You don't need be "perfect" at mindfulness to begin discussing it with your child; you just need to be genuinely interested in the process and honest about your own experience. Whenever you start to feel familiar with the ideas and practices, you can introduce them to your family. Reflect on and discuss your own difficulty sustaining attention, resisting reactivity, and all the rest. This can be an important part of the lesson for your child: you're fallible and yet remain open to trying something new.

As a parent, your job is to prepare your child for the road ahead, rather than endlessly (and impossibly) trying to fix the road itself. You can't predict every potential difficulty and protect your child from every pothole. But if you help your child cultivate mindfulness, he'll develop resilience, improved executive function, and social and emotional skills that allow him to steer himself when the time comes.

The basics for teaching mindfulness are similar to those for many other skills, from art to tennis. Based on your own practice, you've developed some expertise, which you can adapt to engage your child, adjusting the language and practices to be developmentally appropriate. This comes down to making mindfulness real, engaging, and fun, and translating it into terms that will make sense to your child. There are many helpful books on this topic (some are listed in the Resources section).

Here are just a few guidelines on how to approach sharing mindfulness with your child in an age-appropriate way. Specific suggestions follow, but more important than a checklist of specific practices is a sense of what mindfulness really means.

- **For preschoolers**, mindfulness is often introduced through play. In fact, free play itself has been linked with the development of executive function (Barnett et al. 2008). One program, called Tools of the Mind, emphasizes games that help children cultivate self-control without any formal discussion of mindfulness.

- **For children in early elementary school**, some discussion of concepts related to mindfulness becomes possible, but the emphasis remains on games and activities. Formal practices can be introduced, perhaps as play. Mindfulness-based activities that include physical exercise, like yoga or martial arts, may feel more accessible than sitting still.

- **For preadolescents and teens**, the same approach you've taken as an adult is effective, although the practices should be shortened and the language should be adapted into their vernacular.

The following sections provide guidance on introducing different aspects of mindfulness to children, with three ways to highlight each for your child:

- **Demonstrate it.** Start by demonstrating the skill in yourself. As you do so, notice if you get frustrated with your own inconsistency. When that happens, start over again, with patience and self-compassion.

- **Establish it as a daily practice.** Introduce your child to mindfulness practice and create new routines to support practicing mindfulness amidst the bustle of family life.

- **Emphasize it in everyday life.** Emphasize informal mindfulness through activities together, discussions, and books that focus on the traits you choose.

Paying Attention

The starting point for mindfulness is paying attention to life while it happens, rather than living on autopilot. All parents wish their kids would pay attention more often. But telling them to pay attention isn't nearly as effective as *showing* them. Cultivating attention requires daily, long-term effort.

Demonstrate It

- Give your child your full attention. Turn off distractions and emphasize spending time together. Work at being fully present for family meals and playtime, and capitalize on times like waiting for the bus or at doctor appointments.

- Encourage your child to devote complete attention to any given activity. Discuss each of the five senses as you do things together. Cooking and eating are great avenues for cultivating attention in children, as is going for a walk or hike. Articulate your own experience and encourage your child to do the same.

Establish It as a Daily Practice

- Teach your child adapted versions of the formal practices in this book. Many meditations work well for kids if simply shortened, such as spending just a minute or two paying attention to what breathing feels like.

- Use the Fifteen Breaths practice. Encourage your child to count fifteen slow breaths, perhaps as a way of settling himself when flustered. This practice can also ease transitions, such as sitting down for a meal or getting ready for bed. Explain that distractions happen, and gently encourage him to just notice this and then come back to the practice without judging himself as bad.

- Use play-based instruction for younger children. Many fun activities can be used to guide attention, such as blowing bubbles and observing them until they pop, or aiming to listen only to music that's playing and not other sounds.

- When your child seems frustrated, don't demand that he calm down or focus; use an attention practice to guide him. Without finger-pointing ("Take a breath already!"), see if your child settles when given a focus other than his agitated thoughts. There's a subtle difference between telling someone to calm himself and encouraging him to focus attention elsewhere instead.

- Here are a couple more possibilities for working with attention in young children:

  - Have your child place a stuffed animal on his belly and rock it to sleep with each breath. Older children may prefer using a pebble or putting their hand on their belly instead.

  - For a very young child, ask him to blow toward your hand. For five breaths, pretend each slow breath extends one finger. Then, with a second set of five breaths, have each breath bring one finger down again.

Emphasize It in Everyday Life

- Point out, without judgment, when your child has become focused on the past or future instead of the moment. Validate your child's concerns while guiding him back to what can be done in this moment: "What happened sounds really painful. What can we do about that now?" "Sounds like you're really worried about the game next weekend. Would you like to go out and practice shooting hoops?"

- Prioritize activities that build attention and sustain focus, from imaginative play to martial arts, chess, or yoga. Minimize activities that affect attention for the worse, like watching television or playing video games.

Responsiveness

As they grow, children gain skill in pausing and reflecting before acting, though many don't fully develop this capacity until after adolescence. ADHD hinders this process. One way to decrease reactivity in children is mindfulness practice, which builds responsiveness.

Demonstrate It

- Display responsiveness yourself. When you get visibly caught up in an emotion, use it as an opportunity to show your child that it's possible to notice that experience and then settle yourself. You can even describe your agitated moments as they happen: "I'm feeling pretty angry right now. I'm going to take a break, and then we can talk later." If there's a mindfulness practice you find useful, let your child see you use it to settle yourself.

Establish It as a Daily Practice

- Introduce child-friendly guided practices and do them with your child. Mindfulness practice encourages observing, pausing, and then responding to whatever comes up, making these skills more easily accessible in day-to-day life. Several of the books listed in the Resources section include guided practices for children.

- Use the STOP practice frequently until it becomes a routine. Encourage this habitual pause without adding judgment to the situation: "Use your $#*@^ STOP practice now. You know better!"

Emphasize It in Everyday Life

- Patiently guide your child toward responsiveness. Instead of meeting intensity with intensity, return to your intentions around communication recorded in the exercises in chapter 5. Aim yourself toward words and actions that de-escalate situations.

- When your child feels stressed or ready to lash out, guide him toward ways to manage his feelings. Use targeted praise, rewards, and the other approaches you've learned in this book to assist him in developing the life skill of responsiveness. During quiet times, discuss appropriate ways to handle challenging moments.

- Demonstrate responsiveness around your child's ADHD. Right now, today, remind yourself of the executive function differences involved in ADHD. Focus your attention—and your child's—on what's gone well, what progress he's made, and his strengths.

Awareness of the Body

A frequently overlooked aspect of experience is the physical sensations and sounds present at any moment. Becoming more aware of emotions and stress (and noticing them sooner) often grows from increasing awareness of physical experience. In addition, body sensations may serve as a focal point when building attention.

Demonstrate It

- Describe your own experience, noting sights, smells, and sounds.

- Point out the physical side of emotions and connections between emotions and the body.

Establish It as a Daily Practice

- Teach your child the body scan from chapter 10 to increase his awareness of his physical experience. As part of a bedtime routine, it can help your child settle his mind and body while also providing an accessible way to schedule mindfulness.

Emphasize It in Everyday Life

- Use sound to focus attention. One easy approach is to sound a tuning fork or bell and ask your child to raise his hand when he can no longer hear the tone.

- Use a phone app that chimes a bell at random times during the day to signal everyone in your family to pause and check in when they hear the sound.

Awareness of Thoughts

Thoughts can, of course, be useful and require action, and they also tend to feel quite solid to children—even ones like *There's a monster under my bed!* Seek balance between validating anxious thoughts and a discovery that not at all are based in reality.

Demonstrate It

- Label your own mental habits. In an unforced manner and without pointing fingers, discuss the fact that not every thought is worthy of attention: "I notice that sometimes I think I'm not very good at this game, and it makes me want to give up."

- Notice your own language around problem behaviors and aim to communicate in ways that support your intentions. One common habit is to label people instead of actions. "You're bad" means something very different from "You acted badly." The first suggests the thought that your child is fundamentally flawed; the second recognizes a behavior to address.

Establish It as a Daily Practice

- Use the exercise Watching the Weather, from chapter 4, to allow your child to directly experience that many thoughts come and go on their own: "The brain makes thoughts all the time, but we don't have to believe everything we think."

Emphasize It in Everyday Life

- Explain that nearly all of us have an inner critic—an unkind voice chattering away in the mind—and how easy it is to take what it says at face value and believe it to be true. Also point out the human tendency to be quick to blame ourselves or others when something goes wrong. For children who are struggling with ADHD, it can be easy to believe self-critical thoughts such as *I'm no good at school.* Help your child notice this when it happens, label it, and then focus on strengths instead.

- Explain that negative thoughts are sticky—that the mind tends to tenaciously hold on to them. For older children, explore the connection between training in focused attention and guiding ourselves away from negative thoughts more easily. Part of stress is simply that something unsettling grabs our attention and we have a hard time letting go of it.

Awareness of Emotions

The act of describing emotions has inherent value for children, in part by building emotional intelligence. Emotions keep us safe by indicating when we feel at risk, but like thoughts, they can occur for less meaningful reasons, such as sleeping poorly. Guide your child in becoming more aware of his emotional world, being able to describe it, and feeling comfortable with the full range of human feelings. Let him know that all emotions are normal and that whatever he feels is okay, but the more he talks about his emotions, the less they'll run his life.

Demonstrate It

- Describe your emotions and allow your child to share in your emotional experience. You may need to shelter your child from particularly intense emotions you experience—at least until you settle yourself. But in general, he'll learn from hearing how you understand your emotions: "I was so excited to see you on stage; it made me happy." "What that man said at the store made me really angry."

Establish It as a Daily Practice

- Encourage your child to verbally label what he feels either during or after mindfulness practice.

- Create a practice around describing emotions in everyday life and exploring how your child feels emotions in his body. Bring creativity to the practice, describing emotions with colors or other attributes (heavy, light, tingly) that make them seem more concrete.

Emphasize It in Everyday Life

- Assist your child in describing his emotions. Validate his experience of his emotions while also explaining that he can feel whatever he feels but still choose how to act: "I see that you're angry, but you can't throw your toys."

- Use books that describe emotions. Many picture books describe and illustrate emotions for children (several are listed in the Resources section).

Building Compassion and Gratitude

Mindfulness affects how we relate to the world. You can use mindfulness to guide your child toward more empathy, compassion, and gratitude, and also toward recognizing that suffering drives the behavior of even the people we disagree with most.

Demonstrate It

- Show your child compassion for others. Interact with the world as you'd like your child to. Without overwhelming yourself with the responsibility, realize that your child learns from how you talk to a cashier, coach, teacher, or anyone else.

- Show appreciation for whatever you have, however big or small it seems at any particular point in time.

Establish It as a Daily Practice

- Create a daily gratitude practice. Near dinnertime or bedtime, take a moment to reflect on the day with your family. Have every family member list several things that happened to be thankful for.

- Reinforce the idea of wishing oneself and others well. As your child becomes more familiar with mindfulness, considering adding a loving-kindness practice. Instead of the traditional phrases, you might use only "May I feel happy" or the image of a hug from a grandparent.

- Make a game of tracking what it took to get an item of food or a toy to your child, and give thanks. "How many people do you think were involved in creating this toy and getting it to your playroom?" Guide your child in exploring the facets: someone collected the materials, someone took them to the factory, someone designed the toy, someone built the toy, someone packaged it, someone shipped it, and someone finally bought it for your child.

Emphasize It in Everyday Life

- Explain that even misbehavior is usually driven by fear, hurt, misunderstanding, or some other form of suffering. Of course, make sure your child understands that this doesn't mean he has to tolerate bullying or other unkind behavior, and that in such situations, it may be best to leave the situation and seek adult support. Afterward, there may be space in the discussion to recognize that even bullying probably arises from suffering.

- Simply reading fiction may be helpful, as it's been shown to build compassion and increase the ability to take the perspective of others (Mar, Oatley, and Peterson 2009).

Practice: Breathing Compassion

As this book draws to a close, let's remain with the final aspect of mindfulness outlined previously: compassion. At times we feel entirely connected to our sense of compassion for ourselves or others: someone we love, a friend, someone in crisis, or even someone we hardly know. Through the loving-kindness meditation in chapter 9, we can even cultivate compassion for those we find difficult. Yet all too often, we get swept up in the everyday challenges of life and lose touch with our sense of compassion, even for our children. One way to bring yourself back onto more solid ground is with an in-the-moment mindfulness practice.

At any time in everyday life, you can bring wishes for others' well-being fully into your awareness, just as you do during formal loving-kindness meditation. You can acknowledge when someone is suffering and wish them relief. You can return to your best intentions in even just one breath.

Anytime you find yourself caught up in difficult interactions, you can take a moment to remind yourself that, beneath surface struggles or conflicts, everyone is driven by an inner desire to avoid suffering and find a measure of peace. Then, in the midst of that difficult moment, bring your attention to your breath. As you breathe in, recognize the distress in yourself, your child, or whomever you're dealing with. And as you breathe out, offer your best intentions: kindness, patience, strength, lightness… That's it. That's all there is.

To see how this works in real life, consider this example: You and your child begin wrestling over homework, bedtime, or curfew. Right then, as it happens, breathe in and recognize your child's distress. Then breathe out and focus on offering back wisdom, calm, or whatever else feels right to you: *I see that you're upset and I wish with all my heart for you to be happy.* When your child has you rattled, this practice can serve as a reminder of how you'd like to guide yourself through these challenging moments: *I truly wish you happiness…even though you are rolling on the floor making a scene.*

At the same time, you can take care of yourself. Notice your own distress, such as feelings of being overwhelmed or frustrated. That's real too. Then, breathing in, note your swirling thoughts and emotions. And breathing out, express your wishes for yourself: balance, strength, patience… whatever fits. You can sustain this focus with specific phrases if you like: *May I be happy and live my life with ease.* Alternatively, you can emphasize concepts that define your larger intentions. *Breathing out, I offer myself wisdom and joy.* You can also offer yourself concrete, specific reminders: As you breathe in, note your state: *I feel angry.* And as you breathe out, recall your intentions: *I remind myself to smile.*

You can extend this same kind of recognition and compassion to anyone, even people you don't know or with whom you disagree. You can do it anytime and anywhere: at a family gathering, during a school meeting, or when standing in line at the grocery store. Breathing in, acknowledge all the suffering of those around you; and breathing out, offer back compassion.

Mindfulness, the Brain, and Family Well-Being

As discussed, recent findings in neuroscience have revealed that neuroplasticity—influencing how the brain is wired—is possible throughout the life span. Change is always possible. Notice any tendencies to believe otherwise, particularly by categorizing yourself, your child, or your family and thereby circumscribing your life: *I will always have a temper. My child will always be scattered. We will never be able to stick to that new routine.*

Let go of assumptions about where you should be with ADHD or mindfulness right now and instead focus on your intentions. Commit to building the traits you'd like to develop—as a parent and in your child. With persistence and dedication, growth inevitably follows.

As you've undoubtedly discovered, everything changes when you start paying attention. You can pause long enough to see your mental and emotional habits and typical patterns of reacting. You can notice tendencies to get lost in the future or past and return yourself to the moment. You can see life more clearly, as it is, and bring more intention to facing whatever is happening. You can choose to respond to your experience, instead of reacting, and in those inevitable moments when you fail to do so, you can give yourself a break.

Along the way, you're rewiring your brain: *That's me avoiding conflict again. I need to pause, reflect, and revisit my intentions… Okay, this time I'm going to try something different.*

The reality is that your child has ADHD, and you and your family are living with it. It affects your child's experience and your own, and challenges you by disrupting daily activities, relationships, and your child's education in many ways. But through practical and compassionate decision making, you've been overcoming these problems and forging a new path forward for yourself and your child.

Mindfulness is giving you tools not just for overcoming ADHD, but for living a life of happiness and well-being. At any moment you may feel happy or sad. You'll continue to have both positive and negative experiences. But as you find it easier to settle yourself, manage your stress, and live life more fully, you, your child, and your family will experience the happiness, ease, and well-being you all deserve.

Action Plan: Establishing and Sustaining a Mindfulness Practice

When you practice mindfulness consistently, the traits you develop become more easily accessible throughout your life. It's natural to run into some hurdles along the way. Each time you notice this happening, recommit and start again.

As a reminder of why you'd like to practice mindfulness, write down the skills and traits you'd like to develop through your practice:

_____

_____

_____

☐ Commit to a daily formal mindfulness practice for yourself and your child. Schedule it and set up reminders:

☐ My plan for myself:

_____

_____

☐ My plan for my child:

_____

_____

☐ Reinforce mindfulness through everyday informal practice, and create reminders to help you stay on track with this as well:

    ☐ Post reminders to do the STOP or Fifteen Breaths practice.

    ☐ Choose a few informal practices, such as eating, walking, or paying full attention to an activity with your child, and commit to practicing at least one each day. Write those activities here:

_____

_____

_____

☐ Take a local mindfulness class or join a mindfulness group.

☐ Read other books on mindfulness. For a few suggestions, see the Resources section.

Resources

Rating Scales

Adult ADHD Self-Report Scale: http://www.hcp.med.harvard.edu/ncs/ftpdir/adhd/18Q_ASRS_English.pdf

Childhood ADHD Rating Scales (available through your school, pediatrician, or psychologist): Vanderbilt, Conners, Brown, SNAP, Behavioral Rating Inventory of Executive Functioning (BRIEF), Barkley Executive Function Scales

Books

Mindfulness

Happiness Is an Inside Job, by Sylvia Boorstein

A Mindfulness-Based Stress Reduction Workbook, by Bob Stahl and Elisha Goldstein

Mindful Eating, by Jan Chozen Bays

The Mindful Way Through Depression, by Mark Williams, John Teasdale, Zindel Segal, and Jon Kabat-Zinn

Practicing Peace in Times of War, by Pema Chödrön

Real Happiness: The Power of Meditation, by Sharon Salzberg

Wherever You Go, There You Are, by Jon Kabat-Zinn

Guiding Children in Mindfulness

Child's Mind: Mindfulness Practices to Help Our Children Be More Focused, Calm, and Relaxed, by Christopher Willard

The Mindful Child: How to Help Your Kid Manage Stress and Become Happier, Kinder, and More Compassionate, by Susan Kaiser Greenland

Planting Seeds: Practicing Mindfulness with Children, by Thich Naht Hahn

Sitting Still Like a Frog, by Eline Snel

A Still Quiet Place: A Mindfulness Program for Teaching Children and Adolescents to Ease Stress and Difficult Emotions, by Amy Saltzman

Children's Books Related to Mindfulness

Alexander and the Terrible, Horrible, No Good, Very Bad Day, by Judith Viorst

The Mindful Teen, by Dzung Vo

No Ordinary Apple: A Story About Eating Mindfully, by Sara Marlowe

Peaceful Piggy Meditation, by Kerry Lee MacLean

Smile a Lot!, by Nancy Carlson

When Sophie Gets Angry—Really, Really Angry, by Molly Bang

Zen Shorts, by Jon J. Muth

Promoting Good Sleep Habits

Healthy Sleep Habits, Happy Child, by Marc Weissbluth

What to Do When You Dread Your Bed: A Kid's Guide to Overcoming Problems with Sleep, by Dawn Huebner

General ADHD and Parenting Books

The ADHD Explosion: Myths, Medication, Money, and Today's Push for Performance, by Stephen Hinshaw

Basic Facts About Dyslexia and Other Reading Problems, Louisa Moats

The Blessing of a Skinned Knee: Using Jewish Teachings to Raise Self-Reliant Children, by Wendy Mogel

The CHADD Educator's Manual on Attention-Deficit/Hyperactivity Disorder, edited by Chris Dendy

Making the Grade with ADD: A Student's Guide to Succeeding in College with Attention Deficit Disorder, by Stephanie Sarkis

Adult ADHD

The ADHD Marriage Effect, by Melissa Orlov

Is It You, Me, or Adult ADD?, by Gina Pera

The Mindfulness Prescription for Adult ADHD, by Lidia Zylowska

More Attention, Less Deficit, by Ari Tuckman

Taking Charge of Adult ADHD, by Russell Barkley

Mindfulness Apps

Get Some Headspace

Insight Timer

Mindfulness Bell

Stop, Breathe & Think

Calm (and calm.com)

Smiling Mind

References

Alizadeh, H., and C. Andries. 2002. Interaction of parenting styles and attention deficit hyperactivity disorder in Iranian parents. *Child and Family Behavior Therapy* 24: 37–52.

American Psychiatric Association. 2013. *Diagnostic and Statistical Manual of Mental Disorders*, 5th edition. Washington, DC: American Psychiatric Association.

Arnold, L., J. Swanson, L. Hechtman, B. Vitiello, B. Molina, P. Jensen, S. Hinshaw, and T. Wigal. 2008. The MTA: Understanding the 36-month follow-up findings in context. *Attention*, April: 20–25.

Atkins, M. S., W. E. Pelham, and M. H. Licht. 1985. A comparison of objective classroom measures and teacher ratings of attention deficit disorder. *Journal of Abnormal Child Psychology* 13(1): 155–167.

Barkley, R. 2006. *Attention-Deficit/Hyperactivity Disorder: A Handbook for Diagnosis and Treatment.* New York: Guilford.

Barkely, R. 2010. *Taking Charge of Adult ADHD.* New York: Guilford.

Barkley, R. A. 2014. Sleep problems and ADHD—An overview. *ADHD Report* 22: 6–11.

Barnett, W. S., K. Jung, D. J. Yarosz, J. Thomas, A. Hornbeck, R. Stechuk, and S. Burns. 2008. Educational effects of the Tools of the Mind Curriculum: A randomized trial. *Early Childhood Research Quarterly* 23: 299–313.

Beck, J., M. Gerber, S. Brand, U. Puhse, and E. Holsboer-Trachsler. 2013. Executive function performance is reduced during occupational burnout but can recover to the level of healthy controls. *Journal of Psychiatric Research* 47: 1824–1830.

Biederman, J., S. V. Faraone, E. Mick, T. Spencer, T. Wilens, K. Kiely, J. Guite, J. S. Ablon, E. Reed, and R. Warburton. 1995. High risk for attention deficit hyperactivity disorder among children of parents with childhood onset of the disorder: A pilot study. *American Journal of Psychiatry* 152: 431–435.

Bloch, M. H., and A. Qawasmi. 2011. Omega-3 fatty acid supplementation for the treatment of children with attention-deficit/hyperactivity disorder symptomatology: Systematic review and meta-analysis. *Journal of the American Academy of Child and Adolescent Psychiatry* 50: 991–1000.

Breznitz, Z. 2003. The speech and vocalization patterns of boys with ADHD compared with boys with dyslexia and boys without learning disabilities. *Journal of Genetic Psychology* 164: 425–452.

Brinkman, W. B., S. N. Sherman, A. R. Zmitrovich, M. O. Visscher, L. E. Crosby, K. J. Phelan, and E. F. Donovan. 2009. Parental angst making and revisiting decisions about treatment of attention-deficit/hyperactivity disorder. *Pediatrics* 124: 580–589.

Brown, P. L. 2007. In the classroom, a new focus on quieting the mind. *New York Times*, June 16.

Brown, T. E. 1996. *Brown Attention-Deficit Disorder (ADD) Scales.* San Antonio, TX: Psychological Corporation.

Brown, T. E. 2006. Inside the ADD mind. *ADDitude Magazine*, April/May.

Carlson, L. E. 2012. Mindfulness-based interventions for physical conditions: A narrative review evaluating levels of evidence. *ISRN Psychiatry* 2012: 651583.

Chödrön, P. 2006. *Practicing Peace in Times of War: A Buddhist Perspective.* Boston: Shambhala Publications.

Chonchaiya, W., and C. Pruksananonda. 2008. Television viewing associates with delayed language development. *Acta Paediatrica* 97: 977–982.

Christakis, D. A., J. Gilkerson, J. A. Richards, F. J. Zimmerman, M. M. Garrison, D. Xu, S. Gray, and U. Yapanel. 2009. Audible television and decreased adult words, infant vocalizations, and conversational turns: A population-based study. *Archives of Pediatrics and Adolescent Medicine* 163: 554–558.

Christakis, D. A., F. J. Zimmerman, D. L. DiGiuseppe, and C. A. McCarty. 2004. Early television exposure and subsequent attentional problems in children. *Pediatrics* 113: 708–713.

Clark, R., P. Kirschner, and J. Sweller. 2012. Putting students on the path to learning: The case for fully guided instruction. *American Educator*, Spring: 6–11.

Cohen, N. J., R. Menna, D. D. Vallance, M. A. Barwick, N. Im, and N. B. Horodezky. 1998. Language, social cognitive processing, and behavioral characteristics of psychiatrically disturbed children with previously identified and unsuspected language impairments. *Journal of Child Psychology and Psychiatry* 39: 853–864.

Conners, C. K. 1998. *The Conners ADHD Rating Scales.* North Tonawanda, NY: Multi-Health Systems.

Courage, M. L., A. N. Murphy, S. Goulding, and A. E. Setliff. 2010. When the television is on: The impact of infant-directed video on 6- and 18-month-olds' attention during toy play and on parent-infant interaction. *Infant Behavior and Development* 33: 176–188.

Czerniak, S. M., E. M. Sikoglu, J. A. King, D. N. Kennedy, E. Mick, J. Frazier, and C. M. Moore. 2013. Areas of the brain modulated by single-dose methylphenidate treatment in youth with ADHD during task-based fMRI: A systematic review. *Harvard Review of Psychiatry* 21: 151–162.

Davidson, R. J., J. Kabat-Zinn, J. Schumacher, M. Rosenkranz, D. Muller, S. F. Santorelli, F. Urbanowski, A. Harrington, K. Bonus, and J. F. Sheridan. 2003. Alterations in brain and immune function produced by mindfulness meditation. *Psychosomatic Medicine* 65: 564–570.

DeLoache, J. S., C. Chiong, K. Sherman, N. Islam, M. Vanderborght, G. L. Troseth, G. A. Strouse, and K. O'Doherty. 2010. Do babies learn from baby media? *Psychological Science* 21: 1570–1574.

Dempsey, A., J. Dyehouse, and J. Schafer. 2011. The relationship between executive function, AD/HD, overeating, and obesity. *Western Journal of Nursing Research* 33: 609–629.

Dendy, C. A. Z., and A. Zeigler. 2003. *A Bird's-Eye View of Life with ADHD: Advice from Young Survivors.* Cedar Bluff, AL: Cherish the Children.

Desbordes, G., L. T. Negi, T. W. Pace, B. A. Wallace, C. L. Raison, and E. L. Schwartz. 2012. Effects of mindful-attention and compassion meditation training on amygdala response to emotional stimuli in an ordinary, non-meditative state. *Frontiers in Human Neuroscience* 6: 292.

Dickstein, S. G., K. Bannon, F. X. Castellanos, and M. P. Milham. 2006. The neural correlates of attention deficit hyperactivity disorder: An ALE meta-analysis. *Journal of Child Psychology and Psychiatry* 47: 1051–1062.

Drayton, A. K., M. N. Andersen, R. M. Knight, B. T. Felt, E. M. Fredericks, and D. J. Dore-Stites. 2014. Internet guidance on time out: Inaccuracies, omissions, and what to tell parents instead. *Journal of Developmental and Behavioral Pediatrics* 35: 239–246.

Eyberg, S., and B. Funderburk. 2011. *Parent-Child Interaction Therapy Protocol.* Gainesville, FL: PCIT International.

Fiese, B., and M. Schwartz. 2008. Reclaiming the family table: Mealtimes and child health and wellbeing. 2014. Available at http://www.yaleruddcenter.org/resources/upload/docs/what/reports/reclaimingfamilytable.pdf. Accessed November 2, 2014.

Flook, L., S. B. Goldberg, L. J. Pinger, and R. J. Davidson. 2014. Promoting prosocial behavior and self-regulatory skills in preschool children through a mindfulness-based kindness curriculum. *Developmental Psychology*, epub ahead of print.

Flook, L., S. L. Smalley, M. J. Kitil, B. M. Galla, S. Kaiser-Greenland, J. Locke, E. Ishijima, and C. Kasari. 2010. Effects of mindful awareness practices on executive functions in elementary school children. *Journal of Applied School Psychology* 26: 70–95.

Garrison, M. M., and D. A. Christakis. 2012. The impact of a healthy media use intervention on sleep in preschool children. *Pediatrics* 130: 492–499.

Gentile, D. A., R. A. Reimer, A. I. Nathanson, D. A. Walsh, and J. C. Eisenmann. 2014. Protective effects of parental monitoring of children's media use: A prospective study. *JAMA Pediatrics* 168: 479–484.

Gilger, J. W., B. F. Pennington, and J. C. DeFries. 1992. A twin study of the etiology of comorbidity: Attention-deficit hyperactivity disorder and dyslexia. *Journal of the American Academy of Child and Adolescent Psychiatry* 31: 343–348.

Gorrindo, T. 2010. Teach teens (and yourself!) how to W.A.I.T. Available at http://apahealthy minds.blogspot.com/2010/08/posting-something-to-your-social.html. Accessed November 2, 2014.

Gottman, J. 2012. The positive perspective: Dr. Gottman's magic ratio! Available at http://www.gottmanblog.com/2012/12/the-positive-perspective-dr-gottmans.html. Accessed November 2, 2014.

Goyal, M., S. Singh, E. M. Sibinga, N. F. Gould, A. Rowland-Seymour, R. Sharma, et al. 2014. Meditation programs for psychological stress and well-being: A systematic review and meta-analysis. *JAMA Internal Medicine* 174: 357–368.

Gunaratana, B. 2014. Bringing the benefits of meditation in daily life. Available at http://bhavanasociety.org/resource/question_benifits_of_meditation_in_daily_life. Accessed November 2, 2014.

Hakanen, J. J., and W. B. Schaufeli. 2012. Do burnout and work engagement predict depressive symptoms and life satisfaction? A three-wave seven-year prospective study. *Journal of Affective Disorders* 141: 415–424.

Halperin, J. M., O. G. Berwid, and S. O'Neill. 2014. Healthy body, healthy mind? The effectiveness of physical activity to treat ADHD in children. *Child and Adolescent Psychiatric Clinics of North America* 23: 899–936.

Harstad, E., and S. Levy. 2014. Attention-deficit/hyperactivity disorder and substance abuse. *Pediatrics* 134: e293–e301.

Harstad, E. B., A. L. Weaver, S. K. Katusic, R. C. Colligan, S. Kumar, E. Chan, R. G. Voigt, and W. J. Barbaresi. 2014. ADHD, stimulant treatment, and growth: A longitudinal study. *Pediatrics* 134: e935–e944.

Hastings, N., and J. Schwieso. 1995. Tasks and tables: The effects of seating arrangements on task engagement in primary classrooms. *Educational Research* 37: 279–291.

Haydicky, J., C. Shecter, J. Wiener, and J. Ducharme. 2013. Evaluation of MBCT for adolescents with ADHD and their parents: Impact on individual and family functioning. *Journal of Child and Family Studies*, August: 1–19.

Hinshaw, S. P., and R. M. Scheffler. 2014. *The ADHD Explosion: Myths, Medication, Money, and Today's Push for Performance*. New York: Oxford University Press.

Hoffman, H. 2004. *Struwwelpeter: Merry Tales and Funny Pictures*. Salt Lake City: Project Gutenberg.

Johnson, J. G., P. Cohen, S. Kasen, and J. S. Brook. 2007. Extensive television viewing and the development of attention and learning difficulties during adolescence. *Archives of Pediatrics and Adolescent Medicine* 161: 480–486.

Kabat-Zinn, J. 1991. *Full Catastrophe Living: Using the Wisdom of Your Body and Mind to Face Stress, Pain, and Illness*. New York: Delta.

Kaplan, B. J., S. G. Crawford, G. C. Fisher, and D. M. Dewey. 1998. Family dysfunction is more strongly associated with ADHD than with general school problems. *Journal of Attention Disorders* 2: 209–216.

Kessler, R. C., L. Adler, R. Barkley, J. Biederman, C. K. Conners, O. Demler, et al. 2006. The prevalence and correlates of adult ADHD in the United States: Results from the National Comorbidity Survey Replication. *American Journal of Psychiatry* 163: 716–723.

Kim, O. H., and K. P. Kaiser. 2000. Language characteristics of children with ADHD. *Communication Disorders Quarterly* 21: 154–165.

Kirkorian, H. L., T. A. Pempek, L. A. Murphy, M. E. Schmidt, and D. R. Anderson. 2009. The impact of background television on parent-child interaction. *Child Development* 80: 1350–1359.

Lazar, S. W., C. E. Kerr, R. H. Wasserman, J. R. Gray, D. N. Greve, M. T. Treadway, et al. 2005. Meditation experience is associated with increased cortical thickness. *Neuroreport* 16: 1893–1897.

Leung, M. K., C. C. Chan, J. Yin, C. F. Lee, K. F. So, and T. M. Lee. 2013. Increased gray matter volume in the right angular and posterior parahippocampal gyri in loving-kindness meditators. *Social Cognitive and Affective Neuroscience* 8: 34–39.

Lewis, B. A., E. J. Short, S. K. Iyengar, H. G. Taylor, L. Freebairn, J. Tag, A. A. Avrich, and C. M. Stein. 2012. Speech-sound disorders and attention-deficit/hyperactivity disorder symptoms. *Topics in Language Disorders* 32: 247–263.

Lieberman, M. D., N. I. Eisenberger, M. J. Crockett, S. M. Tom, J. H. Pfeifer, and B. M. Way. 2007. Putting feelings into words: Affect labeling disrupts amygdala activity in response to affective stimuli. *Psychological Science* 18: 421–428.

Lillard, A. S., and J. Peterson. 2011. The immediate impact of different types of television on young children's executive function. *Pediatrics* 128: 644–649.

Mar, R., K. Oatley, and J. Peterson. 2009. Exploring the link between reading fiction and empathy: Ruling out individual differences and examining outcomes. *Communications* 34: 407–428.

Marlowe, S. 2013. *No Ordinary Apple: A Story About Eating Mindfully.* Somerville, MA: Wisdom Publications.

Mazurek, M. O., and C. R. Engelhardt. 2013. Video game use in boys with autism spectrum disorder, ADHD, or typical development. *Pediatrics* 132: 260–266.

McCarthy, S., N. Cranswick, L. Potts, E. Taylor, and I. C. Wong. 2009. Mortality associated with attention-deficit hyperactivity disorder (ADHD) drug treatment: A retrospective cohort study of children, adolescents, and young adults using the general practice research database. *Drug Safety* 32: 1089–1096.

McInnes, A., T. Humphries, S. Hogg-Johnson, and R. Tannock. 2003. Listening comprehension and working memory are impaired in attention-deficit hyperactivity disorder irrespective of language impairment. *Journal of Abnormal Child Psychology* 31: 427–443.

Millichap, J. G., and M. M. Yee. 2012. The diet factor in attention-deficit/hyperactivity disorder. *Pediatrics* 129: 330–337.

Mindell, J. A., B. Kuhn, D. Lewin, L. Meltzer, and A. Sadeh. 2006. Behavioral treatment of bedtime problems and night wakings in infants and young children. *Sleep* 29: 1263–1276.

Moffitt, T. E., L. Arseneault, D. Belsky, N. Dickson, R. J. Hancox, H. Harrington, et al. 2011. A gradient of childhood self-control predicts health, wealth, and public safety. *Proceedings of the National Academy of Sciences of the USA* 108: 2693–2698.

Morrow, R. L., E. J. Garland , J. M. Wright, M. Maclure, S. Taylor, and C. R. Dormuth. 2012. Influence of relative age on diagnosis and treatment of attention-deficit/hyperactivity disorder in children. *Canadian Medical Association Journal* 184: 755–762.

MTA Cooperative Group. 1999. A 14–month randomized clinical trial of treatment strategies for attention-deficit/hyperactivity disorder. The MTA Cooperative Group. Multimodal Treatment Study of Children with ADHD. *Archives of General Psychiatry* 56: 1073–1086.

Mueller, C. M., and C. S. Dweck. 1998. Praise for intelligence can undermine children's motivation and performance. *Journal of Personal and Social Psychology* 75: 33–52.

Muniz, E. I., E. J. Silver, and R. E. Stein. 2014. Family routines and social-emotional school readiness among preschool-age children. *Journal of Developmental and Behavioral Pediatrics* 35: 93–99.

Neff, K. D. 2003. The development and validation of a scale to measure self-compassion. *Self and Identity* 2: 223–250.

Neff, K. D. 2009. Self-compassion. In *Handbook of Individual Differences in Social Behavior*, edited by M. R. Leary and R. H. Hoyle, 561–573. New York: Guilford.

Neff, K. D., and S. N. Beretvas. 2012. The role of self-compassion in romantic relationships. *Self and Identity* 12: 78–98.

Nhat Hanh, T. 2011. *Planting Seeds: Practicing Mindfulness with Children*. Berkeley, CA: Parallax Press.

Nunez-Smith, M., E. Wolf, H. M. Huang, P. G. Chen, L. Lee, E. J. Emanuel, and C. P. Gross. 2010. Media exposure and tobacco, illicit drugs, and alcohol use among children and adolescents: A systematic review. *Substance Abuse* 31: 174–192.

Polanczyk, G., M. S. de Lima, B. L. Horta, J. Biederman, and L. A. Rohde. 2007. The worldwide prevalence of ADHD: A systematic review and metaregression analysis. *American Journal of Psychiatry* 164: 942–948.

Powers, R. L., D. J. Marks, C. J. Miller, J. H. Newcorn, and J. M. Halperin. 2008. Stimulant treatment in children with attention-deficit/hyperactivity disorder moderates adolescent academic outcome. *Journal of Child and Adolescent Psychopharmacology* 18: 449–459.

Reach Out and Read. 2014. Research findings: A proven early literacy intervention. Available at http://www.reachoutandread.org/why-we-work/research-findings. Accessed November 2, 2014.

Robinson, T. N., M. L. Wilde, L. C. Navracruz, K. F. Haydel, and A. Varady. 2001. Effects of reducing children's television and video game use on aggressive behavior: A randomized controlled trial. *Archives of Pediatrics and Adolescent Medicine* 155: 17–23.

Saltzman, A. 2014. *A Still Quiet Place: A Mindfulness Program for Teaching Children and Adolescents to Ease Stress and Difficult Emotions*. Oakland, CA: New Harbinger.

Scheffler, R. M., T. T. Brown, B. D. Fulton, S. P. Hinshaw, P. Levine, and S. Stone. 2009. Positive association between attention-deficit/ hyperactivity disorder medication use and academic achievement during elementary school. *Pediatrics* 123: 1273–1279.

Schoenberg, P. L., S. Hepark, C. C. Kan, H. P. Barendregt, J. K. Buitelaar, and A. E. Speckens. 2014. Effects of mindfulness-based cognitive therapy on neurophysiological correlates of performance monitoring in adult attention-deficit/hyperactivity disorder. *Clinical Neurophysiology* 125: 1407–1416.

Sciberras, E., K. Mueller, D. Efron, M. Bisset, V. Anderson, E. Schilpzand, B. Jongeling, and J. Nicholson. 2014. Language problems in children with ADHD: A community-based study. *Pediatrics* 133:793.

Singleton, O., B. K. Hölzel, M. Vangel, N. Brach, J. Carmody, and S. W. Lazar. 2014. Change in brainstem gray matter concentration following a mindfulness-based intervention is correlated with improvement in psychological well-being. *Frontiers of Human Neuroscience* 8: 33.

Spencer, T. J., A. Brown, L. J. Seidman, E. M. Valera, N. Makria, A. Lomedico, S. V. Faraone, and J. Biederman. 2013. Effects of psychostimulants on brain structure and function in ADHD: A qualitative literature review of magnetic resonance imaging–based neuroimaging studies. *Journal of Clinical Psychiatry* 74: 902–917.

Stahl, B., and E. Goldstein. 2010. *A Mindfulness-Based Stress Reduction Workbook*. Berkeley, CA: New Harbinger.

Stony Brook University. 2014. What is keeping your kids up at night? Powering down at night will help young students power up during the day. Available at http://www.newswise.com /articles/view/622849/?sc=dwhr&xy=5031942. Accessed November 2, 2014.

Swing, E. L., D. A. Gentile, C. A. Anderson, and D. A. Walsh. 2010. Television and video game exposure and the development of attention problems. *Pediatrics* 126: 214–221.

Wolraich, M. L., E. W. Lambert, A. Baumgaertel, S. Garcia-Tornel, I. D. Feurer, L. Bickman, and M. A. Doffing. 2003. Teachers' screening for attention deficit/hyperactivity disorder: Comparing multinational samples on teacher ratings of ADHD. *Journal of Abnormal Child Psychology* 31(4): 445–455.

Zentall, S. S., K. Tom-Wright, and J. Lee. 2013. Psychostimulant and sensory stimulation interventions that target the reading and math deficits of students with ADHD. *Journal of Attention Disorders* 17: 308–329.

Zylowska, L., D. L. Ackerman, M. H. Yang, J. L. Futrell, N. L. Horton, T. S. Hale, C. Pataki, and S. L. Smalley. 2008. Mindfulness meditation training in adults and adolescents with ADHD: A feasibility study. *Journal of Attention Disorders* 11: 737–746.

Mark Bertin, MD, is a developmental behavioral pediatrician in private practice in Pleasantville, NY. He is assistant professor of pediatrics at New York Medical College, on the faculty of the Windward Teacher Training Institute, and on the editorial board of Common Sense Media. His blog regarding topics in child development, mindfulness, and family is available through huffingtonpost.com, psychologytoday.com, mindful.org, and elsewhere. For information about his online mindfulness classes and other resources, visit www.developmentaldoctor.com.

Foreword author **Ari Tuckman, PsyD,** is a clinical psychologist in private practice in West Chester, PA, specializing in the diagnosis and treatment of ADHD. He presents frequently on ADHD and related topics to both professionals and members of the public.

ÞT
9/15

DATE			